SEEING LOS ANGELES: A DIFFERENT LOOK AT A DIFFE. . . . . . .

SEEING LOS ANGELES:

A Different Look at A Different City

Proceedings of A Conference
at The Bibliothèque Nationale de France
June 15–17, 2006

Edited by GUY BENNETT & BÉATRICE MOUSLI

OTIS BOOKS / SEISMICITY EDITIONS
A Project of the Graduate Writing program
of Otis College of Art and Design
LOS ANGELES ● 2007

©2007 Otis Books / Seismicity Editions

This publication was made possible by a grant
from the City of Los Angeles.

Design and Typesetting: Guy Bennett

ISBN-13: 978-0-9755924-9-6
ISBN-10: 0-9755924-9-1

OTIS BOOKS / SEISMICITY EDITIONS
Graduate Writing program
Otis College of Art and Design
9045 Lincoln Boulevard
Los Angeles, CA 90045

www.gw.otis.edu
seismicity@otis.edu

TABLE OF CONTENTS

Acknowledgments

Over the three years that we worked on this project we met many people on both sides of the Atlantic who accepted to share "their" Los Angeles with us, thus helping to make this project a reality. We are indebted to them, as well as to many organizations without whose aid neither the conference nor this book would have been possible.

First and foremost, we would like to thank François Nida, Director of Cultural Events of the Bibliothèque Nationale de France, whose collaboration on the elaboration of the program as well as on the logistics of the conference was instrumental in its success.

We would also like to thank Sammy Hoi, President, and John Gordon, Provost, at Otis College of Art and Design, and Joseph Aoun, former Dean of the College of Letters, Arts, and Sciences at the University of Southern California, for their support. Many thanks to Sylvie Christophe, Deputy to the Cultural Attaché of the French Consulate in Los Angeles, whose enthusiasm is always a driving force, and to Colin Keaveney, who translated several of the French texts for this publication.

Finally, we are grateful for the financial support of the Bibliothèque Nationale de France, the Cultural Services of the French Consulate in Los Angeles, the USC College of Letters, Arts, and Sciences, the USC Francophone Resource Center, Otis College of Art and Design, and the Cultural Services of the City of Los Angeles.

– *Guy Bennett and Béatrice Mousli,*
Los Angeles, 2007

BÉATRICE MOUSLI | *Introduction*

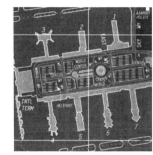

...like earlier generations of English intellectuals who taught themselves Italian in order to read Dante in the original, I learned to drive in order to read Los Angeles in the original.[1]

In the last chapter of *Ecology of Fear*, "Beyond *Blade Runner*,"[2] Mike Davis paints a portrait of Los Angeles in 2019. Not surprisingly, it does look like something right out of Ridley Scott's movie: a desolate, shattered city whose cold, futuristic architecture has been smashed to pieces and whose soul has been poisoned by fear. Applying the chart that Burgess had drawn to visualize the social hierarchy of Chicago in the 1920s, Davis puts the homeless in the center of the city and organizes the remaining Angelenos around them in a series of concentric zones. And he wryly transforms the slogan "Rebuilding L.A." into "padding the bunker."[3]

His Los Angeles is an aggregate of rich and poor ghettos seething with social injustice and interracial hatred, where one's chances for survival are significantly improved with an arsenal of personal weaponry and the protection of neighborhood militias, compared to whom the dreaded members of the LAPD seem as gentle as lambs. In short, it is a city in ruins, one whose communities are engaged in deadly combat against one another in the midst of a state (the "Golden State") that, given the choice, prefers building prisons to funding schools. An avid reader of Bradbury, fascinated by the *Martian Chronicles*, Davis concludes that, if in the '50s Los Angeles could be considered the "global crossroads city," "a modern Alexandria,"[4] the apocalypse is now upon us: "Seen from space, the city that once hallucinated itself as an endless future without natural limits or social constraints now dazzles observers with the eerie beauty of an erupting volcano."[5]

To Davis' bleak vision I prefer the more nuanced view of Jean-Luc

Nancy, whose essay *La Ville au loin* ["The City in The Distance"] is a paean to Los Angeles. Though he shares Davis' perception of L.A. as an elusive metropolis, a place where "the idea, the image of the city has come to be dissolved, stretched to its limits or even *disintegrated* but not suppressed,"[6] he tends to see this in a positive light, describing the city as a fluidity, an open space where "there are barely walls, and thus barely streets."[7] "Far from destroying the city," he writes, "Los Angeles has played on its very essence as an ordinary place: a common place, an absence of place, a non-place, an indefinitely multiplied equivalence of directions and circulations, where dwelling is only a corollary."[8] He sees L.A. as a "capital," a hub of human activity, a living place where, despite the ambient ordinariness, everything seems to transform into a "monument or inscription," elevating the ordinary – and, I would add, the quotidian – to the level of art. This does not erase those contrasts resulting from ethnic and social diversity, as Nancy reminds us, because "Los Angeles is not bourgeois (unlike New York in some neighborhoods), as it is not urban, neither polite nor polished, nor gentle, nor accommodating to the eyes or to the feet." But, "No matter what people say – and they do delight in saying it, so often do people talk about the 'inhospitality' of L.A. – we *can* bump into each other there, get together there, have our favorite spots there."[9]

As the juxtaposition of Davis' and Nancy's Los Angeleses suggest, the city tends to inspire strong reactions, whether hostile or sympathetic. Our goal has been to consider both positions, as well as those in between, exploring the myths and realities of L.A. as seen by Angelenos who dwell in the sprawl, and by visitors drawn to the city for whatever reason. But how do you fit seventeen million people, eight thousand square miles, eighty-eight languages, and just as many religions, cuisines, traditions, etc., into a single poem? How do you present accurate facts and figures for a place in constant flux: three million newcomers each year, somewhat fewer deserters, constant earth movements, recurring natural disasters, and the resultant, inevitable shifts in physical and demographic boundaries?

The authors included in the present volume, whether scholars, writers, poets, or artists, have accepted the challenge to do just that, presenting each in their own way and according to the dictates of their respective disciplines, one or more of the many facets of this kaleidoscopic city. Delineating its material reality and addressing its clichés, examining and/or deconstructing them as the case may be, the texts that follow chart the real and imagined contours of Los Angeles, collectively revealing the current shape of a city commonly referred to as shapeless.

NOTES

1 Reyner Banham, *Los Angeles: The Architecture of Four Ecologies* (New York: Harper & Row, Publishers, 1971) 23.
2 This chapter had just been published in France at the time of the conference in book form, and was of course modeling the latest discourse on Los Angeles between French journalists and intellectuals.
3 Mike Davis, *Ecology of Fear: Los Angeles and the Imagination of Disaster* (New York: Vintage books, 1999) 364.
4 Davis 419.
5 Davis 422.
6 Jean-Luc Nancy, *La ville au loin* (Paris: Editions Mille et Une Nuits, 1999) 11.
7 Nancy 14.
8 Nancy 17.
9 Nancy 19.

KEVIN STARR | *Los Angeles in The World.*
The World in Los Angeles.

In April 1922, to celebrate the inauguration of Rufus Bernhard von KleinSmid as president of the University of Southern California, usc hosted the academic delegates from the Pan-American Congress then being held in Los Angeles. Eight honorary doctorates were awarded to the Pan-American scholars; and in his inaugural address, "A World View of Education," von KleinSmid stressed the intrinsic internationalism of Los Angeles and usc. Here, then, is an interesting paradox. In the very decade in which Los Angeles would become predominately Anglo-American Midwestern in its population and culture, the decade of the Folks, the newly inaugurated president who would transform usc was keying this small Methodist institution, serving a predominately Anglo-Protestant clientele, to internationalism, with special attention being paid to Hispanic America.

Of course, usc had been international from its foundation in 1880, with a Japanese student in its first graduating class. But von KleinSmid was striking a deeper chord, a more persistent pattern, than the mere history of his institution, however important. He was intuiting, directly and immediately, the fundamental formula of Los Angeles, its DNA code if you will, going back to its foundation in September 1781 as a pueblo – which is to say, a full-fledged city, the only such settlement of its kind in Alta California.

Hispanic civilization, first of all, which was bringing Los Angeles into being, was by definition internationalist. To this day, I find it astonishing to contemplate the fact that the Philippines came under

13

Spanish influence in the late-seventeenth century not from Spain itself, but from New Spain, which is to say, from Mexico. To this day, I find it breathtaking to think that New Spain, Mexico, projected itself across the vast Pacific at a time when such a voyage would take more than 200 days and would involve the constant risk of death from shipwreck and/or disease.

There has been a lot of theorizing in the twentieth century – Octavio Paz's great book *The Labyrinth of Solitude* comes immediately to mind – as to the intrinsic internationalism and/or anti-internationalism of Mexico. From one perspective, Mexico looks within, to its interior soul and its own solitary plane of being, where only Mexico exists. Then you have the other side of the Mexican imagination: the Vice Royalty of New Spain which spent the 1500s and the 1600s projecting itself into the vast Pacific; the Jesuits of New Spain who projected themselves north in Mexico, into Arizona, into Baja California, a century and a half ahead of subsequent settlement; the Mexico of Archduke Maximilian's daydream, a royalist Euro-Mexico: dreams that came to naught on the battlefield of Cinco de Mayo.

And, of course, the establishment of Los Angeles itself in September 1781 as a projection of strategic urbanism. To colonize this vast region of Southern California, New Spain invoked the inevitability of a civic secular culture with the granting of full pueblo status to Los Angeles. Los Angeles would not be a mission, a fort or presidio. It would be a city, gathering unto itself the peoples of the world. Indeed, they were already there among the founders, whose blood lines incorporated Spain, Africa and Meso-America. Walk down the streets of Los Angeles (such as they were) by the 1820s, and you would even encounter people from the Philippines, Manila men they were called or Luzon Indians. Hawaiians would be there as well. By the 1830s, Southern California had emerged at the very epicenter of trade routes that began in Boston, rounded Cape Horn, continued up the coasts of South and Central America, traded manufactured goods for hides and beaver skins acquired from mountain men in the interior, then pushed across the Pacific to Hong Kong.

History, at its most basic, is an interaction between people and geography; and both the peoples and the geography of Southern California and its capital city were internationalists, despite the scarcity of settlement in that era and the relatively undeveloped pastoral nature of its material culture.

Between World War I and World War II, the City of Angels was in many ways an Anglo-American enclave. Indeed, the re-founders of the city in the early-twentieth century – the oligarchy that built the aqueduct, brought in the water, crisscrossed the Los Angeles plain with Big Red Cars, got rich as more than 3 million immigrants poured into the region – were fond of saying that Los Angeles would be, most likely, the last major English-speaking city to be established on the planet. They were wrong, of course. They could not have foreseen Las Vegas, Phoenix, and Houston; but those cities are, in a fundamental way, projections of the Los Angeles model onto other Southwestern landscapes.

The point is: even as Los Angeles was being trumpeted as the whitest city in the nation – to the point that only Caucasians were allowed to work on the aqueduct – a more persistent identity was asserting and re-asserting itself in terms of the people of the city. Boyle Heights – as USC history professor George Sanchez will soon be showing in a brilliant new monograph – was among the most international of urban settlements in the country, a sort of Lower East Side for the City of Angels. There was never a time when Los Angelenos ceased enjoying Mexican food, as if the very act of digging into an enchilada contained within itself some form of historical memory, some ritual connection through cuisine with an impending future.

From this perspective, the ethnically monolithic decades of Los Angeles – beginning just before World War I and ending after World War II – will be seen as a mere interval in the larger historic identity of the city as international settlement.

Today, of course, that internationalism has been compounded and re-compounded through immigration and projected and re-projected through technology. Among other identities, Los Angeles is a ranking

Mexican, Korean, Armenian, Iranian, Ethiopian, Chinese, and Native American city. Yes, Native Americans. Metropolitan Los Angeles has the largest population in the nation of urban Americans of Native American descent. It is also an epicenter of Jewish civilization, made that way by both the German-Jewish founders of American Los Angeles in the 1850s, the eastern European immigrants of the late-nineteenth and early-twentieth century, and the refugees, the talented elite of émigrés, who fled to this city in the 1930s, escaping Nazi Europe, enlivening this city with the best of Vienna and Berlin.

This story reinforces an important point about the émigrés of the 1930s and 1940s. You could come to Los Angeles and sustain multiple states of consciousness. Thomas Mann, for example, could settle in Pacific Palisades and still write *Dr. Faustus* (1947), arguably the greatest German-language novel of the twentieth century. Freddie Kohlner, by contrast, could arrive in Los Angeles not speaking a word of English, and within a few short years be writing the novel *Gidget*, filled with the special argot of teenage surfers, which he absorbed from his Los Angeles-born surfing daughter.

It was part of the formula of Los Angeles – and by extension, most of Southern California – that you did not have to shed your identity when you came here. You made contact with a common culture, based on the English language, based on the legal, political, and cultural framework of the region, but you also could sustain, simultaneously, who you were, where you had come from. From this perspective, the internationalism of Los Angeles, present from the beginning, helped pioneer a new model, a new process, whereby the peoples of the world could become American, full citizens of the Republic and the State of California, while also residing in other cultural traditions. In times past, identities had to be left behind when you came to the United States. One assimilated to a predominately Anglo-American cultural point of view. In Los Angeles, by contrast, you became a good American by connecting with the common culture while also remaining who you were.

The British historian Arnold Toynbee uses the word ecumenopolis to describe this phenomena: the ability of a high urban civilization, that is, to bring into ecumenical interface various cultural traditions within the matrix of a shared urban culture. Obviously, Los Angeles is not alone in doing this. New York and Chicago have done it quite successfully as well. But that is precisely the point. Los Angeles is not an exception to American cities, nor is Southern California an exception to American civilization. (And here I respectfully disagree with the great Carey McWilliams.) They are the cutting edge.

It is the destiny of the United States, most of us agree, to become an integrated ecumenical world culture within the constitutional framework conferred on us by the founding fathers and within the cultural matrix created by more than two centuries of American life. When this recognition first dawned, there were many who reacted in fear, who claimed that the forces of irredentism were being unleashed in the Republic. The death in action in Iraq of Thailand-born, Guatemala-born, and Mexico-born United States Marines would seem to dispel that notion.

At his April 1922 inauguration, Rufus Bernhard von KleinSmid also advanced the notion that not only was Los Angeles internationalist in its geo-political identity, it would also, eventually, play a role in the shaping of American foreign policy. How it would have pleased President von KleinSmid to witness the distinguished career of Warren Christopher as secretary of state together with the flourishing nature of this World Affairs Council. But another form of diplomacy, of international relations, is even more conspicuously being driven by Los Angeles: the diplomacy of culture through the entertainment industry, the diplomacy of commerce through the trading partners of Los Angeles, the subliminal internationalism of the great world religions flourishing here and, finally, a kind of social diplomacy being exercised by a society whose every dimension – business, law, entertainment, education, trade, travel – is multinational in content and extent. From this perspective, merely to be in Los Angeles, merely to do business here, is by definition to enter the international community.

Perhaps that is why the *Los Angeles Times* pours so much of its resources into foreign affairs. Perhaps that is why the study of international relations is so conspicuously flourishing at our local colleges and universities. Perhaps that is why we produced Ralph Bunche and Warren Christopher. The very formula, the very DNA code of Los Angeles has been internationalist in one way or another since September 1781.

CYNTHIA GHORRA-GOBIN | *Urban Forms*
and Migrations to Los Angeles

© RMcN

Choice of Approach

Every city can be understood as both a material entity with its own specific shape and a social and political entity. Fustel de Coulanges, the historian of the nineteenth century, noted that unlike the Ancients who had two words (*urbs et civitas*) that explicitly referred to these two aspects of the city, the French language only has one: *ville*. Studying the city means taking into account both its physical and social/political/cultural dimensions, as well as the dialectical relationship between the two. Following the approach outlined by Fustel de Coulanges, I shall explain the structure of Los Angeles via an analysis of the social and cultural changes that have come about as a result of migration to the city. This analysis will stress cultural geography, thus distinguishing itself from a more traditional geographical approach, in which the city's contours tend to be explained more in terms of the lay of the land, the dynamics of population growth combined with economic activity, the city's position relative to networks of exchange and migration, as well as means of transport and their related infrastructure.

Throughout the twentieth century, up until the 1980s and '90s, Los Angeles was often described as "unique" among cities due to its low population density (even in its ghettos and barrios),[1] its centerless urban model (in which no distinction is made between city and suburb), its urban sprawl, its uniform green landscape, and its lifestyles predicated upon the car as a quasi-universally-available means of transportation. As a result, L.A.'s urban model became almost synonymous with "drive-in culture" notwithstanding the fact that, at the end of the nineteenth century, the city had a remarkable public transport system that combined tram (streetcar) and train, which was in part responsible for the city's sprawl. While not denying the unique suitability of its vast coastal plain to urban expansion, the rise of the automobile in the early part of the century, not to mention the construction of a huge freeway network,[2] my explanation of the city's spatial organization will focus on the history of immigration and on images of the city that became common currency among American migrants, arriving first by train from the East Coast, and then later by car from the Midwest.[3] This approach will allow us to anticipate future changes in the shape of L.A. based upon the nature of contemporary immigration.

An Anglo-American Town or the Originality of Immigration to L.A. (Compared to Cities on the East Coast)

At the time of its absorption into the American federation, L.A. was a small Mexican town of 1600 inhabitants, mostly *Californios* – either mixed-race Indians or mixed-race whites. However, in the wake of successive domestic migrations, the city quickly became an Anglo-American outpost on the Pacific coast. The newly arrived settlers were strong believers in the dominant ideology of the day, which was that of "White Protestant America."[4] These Americans also had strong ideas about what an American city should be: one utterly unlike the dense ones they had known on the East Coast. Density was perceived in terms of the housing stock (apartment buildings), the overcrowded atmosphere of poor neighborhoods, and the congested traffic.

Migration to L.A.: the Breakdown

Having been linked by rail to San Francisco, and thus to the rest of the country, Los Angeles began to see an inflow of migrants from the 1880s, and particularly the 1890s, on. Between 1920 and 1930, two million Americans settled in California, 1.5 million of them in the L.A. region, and 100,000 in L.A. itself.[5] L.A.'s population tripled in ten years. With the population boom, real estate became one of L.A.'s economic mainstays, after tourism, agriculture (L.A. and Orange Counties), oil wells, the movies, and later the aeronautics industry. L.A. is notable in this period for the high levels of property ownership, 35% compared to New York's 12%, an indicator of the lifestyle enjoyed by the predominantly well-to-do middle classes. The American dream entails owning one's own home and garden close to nature.

In 1926, L.A. was also a predominantly white city. Out of a population of 1.3 million, only 45,000 were Latino, 33,000 African-American, and 30,000 Asian. Made up predominantly of Americans of European extraction (from Northern European and British stock), the city was seen as "an interesting experiment for the Anglo-Saxon in America."[6] The mastermind of urban planning in Los Angeles, G. Fordon Whitnall, thus wrote that "L.A. had the opportunity to become a model metropolis, exempt from the mistakes of older American cities." Meanwhile a pastor, Bob Shuler, who saw his mission in terms of a daily battle to preserve the soul of the city, described Los Angeles as a "pure city" because its population was not overwhelmingly foreign: "the last purely American city in the nation: it is the only city which is not dominated by foreigners."[7]

Unlike San Francisco, its rival to the north, L.A. was notable for the presence of a powerful oligarchy that oversaw its economic affairs. But it was also made up of babbitts (a nickname borrowed from Sinclair Lewis's novel and given to newcomers) and regular *folks*, as those most economically disadvantaged were called. There is no "working class" to speak of in the first half of the twentieth century: industry (besides aeronautics) played no role in the economic culture of the city and thus could not give rise to working-class neighborhoods. The tertiary sector was dominant, with entertainment, leisure, and real estate and property development. The ruling classes and the babbitts shared the same leisure pursuits, like playing golf and going to beach clubs, which numbered about 200 in 1927.

Given the particular character of migration to Los Angeles, what drew migrants and what image did they have of the city?[8]

Images Related to the American Dream

At its birth, the American state was relatively uninterested in cities. Economic wealth depended mainly upon agriculture and according to the first census in 1790, only 5% of the population lived in cities. The Founding Fathers also chose to build democracy on a bedrock of rural values.[9] Unlike Europe where the city was seen as the crucible of individual emancipation and a school for democracy, in the American psyche this function was fulfilled by the frontier.[10]

In the mid-nineteenth century, however, this neglect of the city gave way to a debate about what the American city should be as people realized that the age of urbanization and industrialization had well and truly arrived. Thus, intellectuals considered ways in which traditional agrarian values could be reconciled in a democracy with new needs engendered by economic development. It was not long before ministers, domestic feminists, and transcendentalist philosophers were united in a consensus that the single-family dwelling with garden, located close to nature, was the ideal habitat for the American family. The historian Kenneth Jackson studied these three groups in a remarkable study published twenty years ago.[11]

Americans new to L.A. brought with them a notion of an ideal city that owed much to this negative view of density perceived as the source of all social ills (public health as well as traffic). In the Western world, urban theorists subscribed to these views and pushed for residential decentralization along with better public transportation. Thus, from its appearance, the car was seen in Los Angeles as the tool that would make urban decentralization possible.[12]

But, at a time when immigration, mainly from Mexico, Central and South America is transforming the racial and ethnic make-up of the city, in effect making it less "Anglo," what changes in the urban fabric can we discern and describe?

The Effect of Contemporary Immigration

Through a presentation of some changes in the social and urban fabric, it will become clear that a transformation has recently affected both the workforce and the city's neighborhoods.

The Recent Changes

At the end of the twentieth century, the face of Los Angeles was transformed by the flux of economic globalization and became home to a whole new range of people. Los Angeles was no longer seen as a regional center, but became part of the network of global cities like New York, a city that she was coming to resemble by dint of her diverse population and the building of skyscrapers. At the beginning of the 1980s, Los Angeles began putting up skyscrapers, which symbolized its integration into the world of high finance, and gradually became integrated into the global economy thanks in great measure to the intervention of the public sector (the Federal government, the State, and the City), which financed road, port, and airport building projects.[13] Free trade was a boon for Los Angeles.

Los Angeles, a city long thought of as the most Anglo in the United States, began to look more like New York, which had always been home to a large number of people born abroad. David Halle, in a comparative study of Los Angeles and New York, has noted a trend toward convergence in respect of their ethnic and racial profiles (see the table below).[14] New York was, and continues to be, *the* city of foreign immigration and L.A. at present looks very similar in being the destination for many foreign migrants (especially since the change in Federal immigration policies that took place in 1965). Both are major-minority cities, cities where minorities are in fact in the majority. This ethnic diversity is part of an emerging multi-ethnic workforce, sometimes referred to as "immigrant ethnic economies."[15]

L.A.	N.Y.	Population: Racial and Ethnic Make-Up (in %)[16]
47%	27%	Latino
11%	27%	African-American
11%	11%	Asian
31%	35%	White (non-Hispanic)

The city's ethnic and racial diversity is discernible in local politics. In the 2005 mayoral election, there were six candidates in the first round; Villaraigosa got 30% of the vote while Hahn (the incumbent) got 25%. In the run-off, the Hispanic candidate won with 57.8% of the vote, a victory that underscored the importance of political coalitions across racial and ethnic lines.[17]

Los Angeles is also beginning to lose her reputation as an "open-shop" (i.e. largely unionized) town.[18] Three movements are now extremely active within the city: 1) a largely Latino-based labor movement; 2) a community-oriented environmentalist movement; and 3) multiethnic coalition politics. The Los Angeles of the beginning of the twenty-first century looks a lot different to the Anglo town of the beginning of the twentieth.[19]

Moves towards New Uses of Urban Space
East Los Angeles (inhabited today by Mexican-Americans or Chicanos) has undergone a transformation since the 1960s with the departure of European immigrants (in the main from Eastern Europe and the USSR) and the arrival of Mexican-Americans.[20] The changes have been gradual and have not radically transformed the neighborhood: 1) houses are now surrounded by a fence that separates the domestic realm from the street, which was not the case before; 2) laundry is put out to dry in the front- or backyard; and 3) the streets are now full of people. Similar changes are visible in San Fernando Valley neighborhoods that are undergoing a process of gentrification driven by a mainly Latino population.

About ten years ago, the LUF (Latino Urban Forum) was founded. It is a lobby group whose aim is to have local authorities undertake urban infra-structural projects that are better suited to Latino lifestyles.[21] The idea is that Latinos support the provision of public spaces (whether central or just local); that they are used to getting around by public transport; and, as the murals attest, they have an appreciation of urban esthetics.[22] The LUF was behind the creation of the "Evergreen Cemetery Jogging Path" in Boyle Heights (East L.A.), the creation of two parks on the disused industrial sites of Cornfield and Taylor Yards, as well as the South Central Community Farm. In 2003, the LUF organized a conference at USC where the focus was mainly on high density urban planning, street life, and the reclaiming of public spaces by communities. Latinos are very much in favor of the creation of squares and support the building of a city park, similar to Central Park in New York, in the center of L.A. During this forum, the then City counselor from the 14th district, a certain Antonio Villaraigosa, went beyond the traditional single-versus-multifamily debate and made the case for development better suited to what people wanted.

Latinos have gotten behind the New Urbanism (NU) movement (the brainchild of two architects, Andre Duany and Peter Calthorpe, and their teams), which has worked for the past fifteen years to increase the density of urban, suburban, and periurban developments in order to foster a sense of place and a pedestrian- and public transport-friendly environment.[23] In his dissertation written at MIT, Michael Mendez underscores Latino interest in NU. He offers the example of Santa Ana, a town in Orange County, where the population is 80% Latino and whose development has taken place along NU lines. For its part, the catholic community of L.A. hired the architect Rafael Moneo (winner of the 1996 Pritzker Prize) to build the Notre-Dame Cathedral in L.A., which includes a square where the congregation can gather after religious services.

In Los Angeles, due on the one hand to the growth of the population and on the other to the decline of the Anglo and rise of the Latino community, the ideal of the single-family home surrounded by a fenceless garden and set back from the street is less and less in vogue in city building plans.[24] This is seen as a positive development by the architects and planners affiliated with New Urbanism, who argue in favor of an alternative to urban sprawl and for sustainable growth solutions.[25]

Los Angeles Remodels

At the beginning of the American chapter of its history, Los Angeles, located on America's western seaboard, attracted a new population of mainly Anglo-American migrants and its experience of demographic growth was, as a result, utterly different to New York's or other East Coast cities'. These migrants shared a solidly American middle-class standard of living and belief in the urban American dream. They wanted to live in a house with a garden back and front. The particularity of its demographic history offers a plausible explanation for Los Angeles' original urban structure, one which obviates any reference to centrality and avoids technological determinism.

For the past few decades, the composition of the migrant populaton coming to the city has noticeably changed to such an extent that it has led to a real diversification of the population in favor of Latinos.

The social transformation of L.A. shows signs of reshaping the physical structure of the city in response to new ways of using public space. Present-day trends in development policy show a move in the direction of ideas championed by the New Urbanism movement. Public space is set to enjoy a new prominence, a point of view shared by Mike Davis.[26] The redevelopment of Grand Avenue, which stretches from Notre Dame cathedral (in the north) to Wilshire Boulevard, passing by the MOCA, Disney Hall (home to the L.A. Philharmonic) as well as the Dorothy Chandler Pavilion, certainly suggests as much. This thoroughfare should confer on the city's downtown a sense of centrality, as should the park that will be built perpendicular to it.[27] Moreover, there are groups demanding a better range of public transport options, especially buses, for those without a car, while significant funds are being spent on the creation of dedicated bus corridors. Los Angeles is getting a make-over in this beginning of the twenty-first century, as a consequence of new migration flows.

NOTES

1   Los Angeles has no neighborhood with a profile similar to Brooklyn or Harlem in New York.

2   Raynar Banham, *Los Angeles: The Architecture of Four Ecologies* (New York: Harper & Row, 1976).

3   Banham 120.

4   The expression "*White Protestant America*" is historian Kevin Starr's (*Material Dreams: Southern California through the 1920s*, Oxford: Oxford University Press, 1990). See also Robert M. Fogelson, *Los Angeles: The Fragmented Metropolis 1850–1930* (Cambridge, MA: Harvard University Press, 1967) and my own, *Los Angeles, le mythe américain inachevé* (Paris: CNRS Editions, 1997, 2000) (winner of the Prix France-Amériques 1998).

5   Ghorra-Gobin.

6   Ghorra-Gobin 120.

7   Ghorra-Gobin 120.

8   James E. Vance Jr., "California & the search for the ideal," *Annals of the Association of American Geographers* (1972): 185–210, as well as Cynthia Ghorra-Gobin, "De l'idéal pastoral à l'artificialisation du milieu nature: Qu'en est-il de la ville américaine?" *Annales de la Recherche Urbaine* 74 (printemps 1997): 69–74.

9   John L. Machor, *Pastoral Cities: Urban Ideals & the Symbolic Landscape of America* (Madison, WI: University of Wisconsin Press, 1987).

10 Andrew Lees, *Cities Perceived: Urban Society in European & American thought 1820–1940,* (Manchester: Manchester University Press, 1985).

11 Kenneth Jackson, *The Crabgrass Frontier: The suburbanization of the United States,* New York (Oxford: Oxford University Press, 1985) as well as David P. Handlin, *The American Home: Architecture & Society 1815–1915* (Boston: Little, Brown & Company, 1979).

12 Martin Wachs, "The evolution of transportation policy in Los Angeles," *Los Angeles & Urban Theory at the End of the Twentieth Century*, Eds. Allen J. Scott & Soja (Berkeley: UC Press, 1996).

13 Steven Erié, *Globalizing L.A.* (Palo Alto, CA: Stanford University Press, 2004) as well as Roger Keil, *Los Angeles: Globalization, Urbanization & Social Struggles* (New York: John Wiley & Sons, 1998).

14 David Halle, ed., *New York & Los Angeles: Politics, society, and culture, A Comparative view* (Chicago, The University of Chicago press, 2003) 158.

15 Roger Waldinger & Mehdi Bozorgmehr, eds., *Ethnic Los Angeles* (New York: Russel Sage Foundation, 1996).

16 Source: Halle 58.

17 Dowell Meyers, "Probing the Demographic Depth of Villaraigosa's mayoral victory," a publication of the Population, Dynamics Research Group, part of the "School of Policy and Planning Development" (SPPD) at the University of Southern California (USC), May 2005 <www.usc.edu/schools/sppd/research/>.

18 Robert Gottlieb, Peter Dreier & al., eds., *The Struggle for A Livable City: The Next Los Angeles* (Berkeley: UC Press, 2005).

19 Lawrence D. Bobo, Melvin L. Oliver, James H. Johnson & Abel Valenzuela Jr., eds. *Prismatic Metropolis: Inequality in Los Angeles* (Russel Sage Foundation, 2000).

20 James T. Rojas, "The Enacted Environment: The Creation of Place by Mexican-Americans," diss., MIT, 1991.

21 An interesting presentation of this association created by James T. Rojas is to be found on the "Latino Professional Network" (LPN) website.

22 Annick Tréguer, *Chicano: Murs peints aux Etats-Unis* (Paris: Presses universitaires de la Sorbonne Nouvelle, 2000).

23 To learn more about *New Urbanism,* see the site www.cnu.org (Congress for New Urbanism) as well as Cynthia Ghorra-Gobin, *La théorie du New Urbanism : Perspectives et enjeux* (Paris: Ministère de l'Equipement, Centre de Documentation de l'Urbanisme [CDU], 2006).

24 Raul Homero Villa & George J. Sanchez, eds., *Los Angeles & the Future of Urban Cultures,* spec. issue of *American Quarterly* (Baltimore, MD: Johns Hopkins University, 2005).

25 Augustin Berque, Philippe Bonnin & Cynthia Ghorra-Gobin, eds., *La ville insoutenable* (Paris: Belin, 2006).

26 Mike Davis, *Magical Urbanism: Latinos Reinvent The US City* (London: Verso, 2001).

27 Cynthia Ghorra-Gobin, "Los Angeles: Réinventer les espaces publics," *Urbanisme* 346 (janvier 2006).

Translated by Colin Keaveney

GUY BENNETT | *Eight Architectural Miniatures*

for Igor Stravinsky

20858 Pacific Coast Highway

This oceanside-defined,
brutalist balance traffic
blasts rhythms its bays
with motor access pediments
light: an infilled, level sandstone
wall of glass blocks touching
the antiquity-fine, shoreline
grid high as the sea,
an armature glazing
spaces flow-linked by light.

455 Upper Mesa Road

A hillwide view blocks tower
connects this home's steeply
sloping site to monolithic
sprawls' elegantly understated,
elevation-shaped volumes, cladding
plaster-wood copper and zinc-coated
layouts bedrooms bottom as loft
spaces curve to terrace
two room masters.

909 25th Street

The barrel-vaulted volume
hearts the bougainvillea grape
wisteria and trumpet run above
the house from the sun-square
skewed axis the street looks
over to the studio's open, green
stucco trellising visual presence
twist-breaks as bands of compact
color space the lot-lathe light
shafts streaming between
the project's great gardens.

1955 ¹/₂ Purdue Avenue

Earthquake pulses design
striking buildings, absorbing
devices base isolators
cylinder within viscous
substances, smaller units energy
efficiency panels and clad
the floor and walls steel
frames enclose inside
faces' exposed visible interior.

5905 Wilshire Boulevard

This pavilion-exuberant, idiosyncratic
Orientalism structures curving, tower-
clad, aggregate bridges the stairs
elevator as columns triangle bowed
box beams suspended from cable-pale,
green stucco curves organic walls
evoke, paneling angles that face
the softly lit space a quiet ramp snakes.

8687 Melrose Avenue

Built blue to house bright
forms, scale the surrounding,
aroused, float-altered
extension to contrasting
fragments symmetrical green
spandrels rotate away via a
plinth the skylit atrium's cylindrical
hinge-curves wedge in red glass
phases this plaza poured in place.

940 North Mansfield

This sandwiched cement
works' west-towering
glimpse treasure troves props,
offering unexpected, truss-
eruptions of building-filled, blue-
curved structures shape-scattered
detritus makes sense of, as complex
sound lounges casting vaults'
exposed workspaces bridges
stair cross from place to place.

1641 Woods Drive

Floating the city this
house captures, 180 cave-
like, completely glazed
views transform the steel
studded, sun-clad panels that
glow night like space enclosing,
frameless spiral climbs
the mezzanine deck transluces
from the copper dropped ceiling.

BRUCE BÉGOUT | *Homeless in Los Angeles*

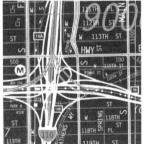

*Of all the underlying forces working toward emancipation of
the city dweller, most important is the gradual reawakening of
the primitive instincts of the agrarian. Agronomy, source of the
ancient wandering tribe.*[1]

For the endlessly beginning twenty-first century, mobility is the only
value that counts. In order to become more mobile, experience needs
to become less material, for the immaterial permits rapid and almost
instantaneous movement akin to that enjoyed by a soul unencumbered
by a body-container. Even places are distinguished by their intrinsic
mobility and modularity. Mobility defines the landscape, modeling
it in its own image, dotting the anonymous expanse with a series
of weigh-stations (drive-ins, railway stations, gigantic supermarkets,
etc.). Los Angeles is the living symbol of the mobile, transient, and
impulsive city, where the "urban" is no longer defined in terms of
buildings and real estate, but rather in terms of the commutes and
journeys that take place every day. Angelenos themselves live in a
virtual and flexible space, both fragile and open-ended, whose only
limits are set by what journeys are feasible. Thus, it is above all traffic
that lends the city its unity. Each inhabitant has a different image
of her city, because she takes a different route to get from place to
place. Each city is the combined sum, not of the points of view of its
inhabitants as Leibniz would have it, but of their wanderings across
the city.

The unchecked expansion of cities makes the relationship between
workplace and home more and more unstable. Each member of the
sedentary community is forced daily, despite herself, to become a
nomad among the throng of her fellows who are also on the move.
It is no accident, then, that the number of stopping-off points –
daily stations of the cross – between these two intangible poles has

increased. The nomad should not be understood as the opposite of the settler, far from being a marginal social figure, she is the very essence of what it means to be a member of society.

A phenomenological approach to this issue is required, which precludes value judgments of the sort that would make urban nomadism synonymous with sterility and an indicator of the unorganic nature of human intelligence. Moreover, wandering in this context is not a traumatic uprooting, as in Spengler's *Decline of the West*, but a rationale characteristic of the evolution of contemporary technology, which aims to facilitate work and ease of movement. It is not the symbol of a murderous separation from Mother Nature, but the realization of human culture's emancipation from nature, in other words from the here-and-now. The "intellectual nomad" thus lives in a state of abstraction, whose primary characteristic is detachment from belonging to any particular place, which might place boundaries on his life and thought. However, with the emergence of infinite urban space, of which Los Angeles is the living exemplar, the big city, by the very virtue of its size, is no longer of such central importance. The very idea of the Big City, as Spengler himself noted, implies separation of city and suburb, capital and region, etc. One of the first effects of contemporary urban space is the breaking down of such barriers, and the homogenization of the city across infinite space, with a consequent loss of distinctions of place and value (this trend sometimes coexists with one that is both an alternative and a reaction: certain points have become designated as places to meet and encounter others, the most recent example of this being café society).

Despite its huge size, the big city remained a tributary of a local rationale (centers, general planning, demarcation, etc.), a legacy from agrarian settlements[2]; meanwhile boundless conurbations are no longer focused on the habitat in terms of localities, but rather in terms of possible interactions and connections, in other words in terms of position and direction. Could it be that the wandering nomad is a throwback in his ways of living and feeling to the hunter-gatherer, "a pure microcosm with neither hearth nor home" (Spengler, *The Decline of the West*)? It is difficult to say, because what he is searching for in his errant existence is no longer anything as simple as nourishment (after all, food outlets are now pretty much everywhere); his quest has more to do with culture, the mind, the exchange and the transmission of information and goods.

The wandering existence also demonstrates that the way of life of the urban nomad does not originate in the emotional cosmopolitanism of the big city, where the individual is a representative of all his fellow beings and a well-defined legal entity. Instead, he belongs to a more fundamental acosmic realm in the sense that he experiences his urban existence without reference to any particular world; without landmarks, whether the natural ones that one might find in a village, or the artificial ones of the Big City. For the *flâneur*, the big city is his world, his microcosm, while the nomad feels no attachment to the urban areas he traverses, for he makes no distinction between here and there. His acosmic state is a result of the fact that space is no longer composed of a series of places with well-defined relationship; nor does it have an orientational coherence. The clear economic and political distinctiveness of place in the big city (visible in striking contrasts between neighborhoods: middle-class and working-class, business and leisure districts, etc.) no longer really exists in American cities, where there is a noticeable breaking down of barriers and where loosely organized zones with random combinations of housing, malls, gas stations, and restaurants have become the norm. Thus, the urban nomad lives in a perpetual state of spatial disorientation, which occasionally inspires fright, but mainly results in a mute stupor at the lack of clarity in the world around him.

Of course, in an apparent effort to compensate for this sense of loss, city dwellers attempt to redefine familiar places in a way that is personally meaningful to them. Thus they distinguish between one street, one district and another; but these fine distinctions are, by their very nature, secondary and constitute a reaction to the undefined essence of urban space. The overwrought aesthetic and architectural style of certain buildings (those belonging to the *googie* style in L.A., for example) as well as the compulsion to define space in terms of favorite places (such-and-such a restaurant, or café, or cinema, etc.) are the direct consequence of the undifferentiated nature of the city, and not the result either of a naturally-occurring impulse to appropriate space or of distinctions made by the city itself in the past.

The wanderer doesn't know where to put himself, where to find his place, and this confusion is the main motif of his endless nomadism. Even without looking at the statistics, which show the number of home moves and job changes have been constantly increasing over the past 20 years in the U.S. and Europe, the irrepressible compulsion among city dwellers for change and movement is patently obvious (both indicators of dissatisfaction with their place). In an urban environment where real estate has less and less to do with dwelling, people are no longer seeking to stay, but are living in a perpetual state of departure. The priority in building developments is ease of passage and the provision of ways of getting around and through for those who are on their way somewhere else.

It is odd that the notion of *Wohnen* (dwelling) as developed by Heidegger in his lecture "Bauen, wohnen, denken," given in Darmstadt on 5 August 1951 as part of the series on "Man and Space," should lead him conceive of every built structure as a potential residence, even extreme cases like the highway, factory, and electricity power station. For him, everything is built with a view to being inhabited:

> The man pulling a trailer with his tractor feels at home on the highway; the mill worker feels at home as she spins; the engineer in charge of the power station feels at home there. These buildings offer Man a place to dwell.

It is at the very least difficult to see how a highway or a power station could be inhabited by workers, even those who could, in some sense, be said to live there; or to consider these architectural forms as the only possible types of human accommodation – Heidegger, who was not quite a Le Corbusier, does not suggest that. More fundamentally however, and contrary to what Heidegger declares, not all man-made constructions are destined to be lived in. From a merely historical standpoint, the first troglodyte dwellings were not built and, similarly, the first structures (enclosures) were not places of residence.

Of course it could be argued that the beginning is not the origin but, without recounting a detailed history of human building that would divert us from our phenomenological approach to the contemporary American city, it is nevertheless safe to say that recent urban development shows that residence is no longer its guiding concern. On the contrary, home building generally follows some basic functional rules and is shaped above all by the materials used, the building's location and the surrounding structures rather than by any meaning imparted during the process of construction. Its essence (if the idea that meaning has essence and substance has any value in this context) is superficial, going no deeper than the buildings' constituent surfaces. In this respect, the American motel and Heidegger's "Black Forest peasant house" (which represented for him the very essence – however much he hated to admit that such a thing existed – of *bauen*, of construction conceived both from the standpoint of and with a view to dwelling) are polar opposites.

However, we owe a debt of gratitude to Heidegger for having explained perhaps better than anyone else that the crisis in lodging is in fact a "crisis in *dwelling*," and that the critical element in human construction lies in the meaning that men can give to *dwelling*. However, it is not certain that the type of dwelling referred to by Heidegger, the peasant house really represents the essence of living (notwithstanding the pains taken by Heidegger to use it only as an example and not a model for future buildings); the essence of man-made constructions is that their foundations only support them once they have been erected. What I mean by this is that the motives for building (of which dwelling is only one and neither the first principle nor the ultimate end) only emerge during the process of erecting structures, so that the justification for building is inherent in the process itself and not necessarily linked to the environment or nature, which it negates by reducing it to mere ground. This is why man's rootlessness is, at bottom, ontological and not a matter of destiny. It is not a historical inevitability, but is instead a component of man's very nature, which is that he has none.

On the other end of the spectrum from the Heideggerian notion of dwelling as the preservation of being is Ralph Waldo Emerson who, as early as the beginning of the nineteenth century, was already giving voice to a very American sense of the importance of the land. As Stanley Cavell has so ably demonstrated,[3] American transcendentalist thought (first and foremost in Emerson and Thoreau) believes in the need to free oneself of everything that is not oneself and, like the hero of Sam Shepard's short story on which Wim Wenders based *Paris-Texas,* to throw off all the borrowed clothing concealing the essential wellsprings of individuality (only this stripping bare can reveal what cannot be disguised) and thus be able, in one's nudity, to commune with the nudity of one's surroundings. Cavell, speaking about the transcendentalists and their feel for the land puts it thus:

> The substantive disagreement with Heidegger, shared by Emerson and Thoreau, is that the achievement of the human requires not inhabitation and sttlement but abandonment, leaving. Then everything depends upon your realization of abandonment. For the significance of leaving lies in its discovery that you have settled something, that you have felt enthusiastically what there is to abandon yourself to, that you can treat the others there are as those to whom the inhabitation of the world can now be left.[4]

Even for Thoreau who spent almost six months alone building his cabin close to Walden Pond in the New England forest, the moral of the experience was that, in the end, such labor (building) is meaningless: "In Arcadia, when I was there, I did not see any hammering stone."[5] Thoreau's Walden experiment was in no way one that championed domesticity. Settling in such a precarious and modest dwelling was rather a way of showing that one should not accord one's residence any importance. Shabby quarters should cure one of the need to set any store by one's home.

On the other hand, he considered that one single act of common sense should be more memorable "than a monument as high as the moon,"[6] and that the pyramids, like all monuments erected by Man, were utterly futile. The house only meant something to him because he built it alone and he abandoned it, refusing to celebrate what no longer had a value once it was detached from its usefulness. It was the act of building that mattered, not the structure itself. As for establishing what the structure should be, it was of little importance. A building's meaning came entirely from its builder, for a "man has no more to do with the style of architecture of his house than a tortoise with that of its shell."[7] What counted more than the house as architectural object was how one domesticated one's self and one's own desires.

This obsession with the self inspires mistrust of any fixture that, in obliging the individual to take up a position, despoiled him of the pure experience of life lived in unbounded mobility. Not even the most straightforward and natural of relationships, i.e. the family, was safe from *Wanderlust*. As Emerson so provocatively put it: "I shun father and mother and wife and brother when my genius calls me. I would write on the lintels of the door-post, Whim."[8]

Even the frontispiece of the dwelling reflected the pointlessness of all fittings, moorings, or forms of permanence. With an identical and profound mistrust of settling down, Thoreau exclaimed in *Civil Disobedience:*

> You must live within yourself, and depend upon yourself always tucked up and ready for a start, and not have many affairs.[9]

The meaning of a building was revealed in the deep need for motiveless and unbridled vacillation, in the cinetic drive that constantly pushed us to go see elsewhere if that is where we were. Social life was thus manifest in caprice, hesitation, and irresolution. To attempt to tame it and give it fixed contours was to denature it. There could be no other closeness to oneself except in oneself, and any attachment constituted a barrier between one's self and itself.

While always attentive to questions of domestic life, the American transcendentalists never hesitated to prize the idea of departure above everything. As important as the building of a house was (and Thoreau spent a year of his life in Walden doing just that), it was nothing compared to the primordial task, which was the "upbuilding of a man."[10] As noble as domestic chores might be (Emerson devoted an essay to them; Thoreau a book), they could not rival the imperious necessity of forming character.

American nomadism, which we find infused in certain forms of urban behavior as well as in the conception of the city, is not merely an effect of the contemporary economic and technical environment; nor is it the result of a loss social points of reference (are they not made to be destroyed?); in fact, behind there is a history that sustains it. In *Thinking of Emerson*, Stanley Cavell considers that not even the status of immigrant is a state Americans should try to escape from, "the catch is that we aspire to this man, to the metamorphosis, to the human."[11] Wandering is not merely the result of a social and historical process; it is, in fact, much closer to human experience in its natural state – technology and urban planning merely give full rein to the possibilities instead of denying them.

In a development that is not devoid of irony, Deleuze and Guattari's concepts of "rhizome" and "deterritorialization" as developed in *Mille Plateaux* (whose avowed goal was to undermine the capitalist and mercantile model of thought by rooting out its deepest emotional and intellectual underpinnings, that is its attachment to territory) have become reality in the remarkable topography of the city that best represents advanced capitalism: Los Angeles. From Bel Air to Watts, the "multiplicity principle" has done its work, weaving webs and building fences, which for once and for all have foregone any reference to a normative whole that could potentially provide an axis or pivot to this wildfire development. Neocapitalism deals very well with unruly sprawl and the rootlessness of people and goods. It smiles upon the incessant movement of capital and merchandise, whose value is not measured by its use-value, but in terms of how easily it can be procured.

Careful attention to maps showing the land use in any American city reveals that two thirds of the ground is unoccupied at any given time, and is free of buildings. City space is made up in the main of roads, parking lots, empty lots; cities are thus in the process of becoming more sparsely built and emptier in order to leave room for movement and parking. However, this desertification of cities (and no longer merely of the countryside) is not due to the abandonment or neglect of pre-existing buildings, but is actually the result of the conscious and deliberate construction of empty space. Man is intentionally injecting urban void into the spaces between buildings. Day after day, Man is inserting gaps between those colored hangars, otherwise known as shopping malls, motels, and department stores. By setting aside space for transit and inactivity, Man is causing urban space to dilate. Why is the city being eviscerated thus in order to inject emptiness at its heart?

The answer lies in the critical prioritization of the flow of goods, the mobility of people, and its essential instrument, the car, which requires of city-dwellers that they become, for all intents and purposes, nomads. As Reyner Banham rightly points out for Los Angeles, is more important than being.[12] It is thus the automobile culture, the motor behind the remodeling of the environment, that is behind this hollowing out of urban space and its attendant behavioral adaptations, which include endless wandering and transit. By nomadism I mean a way of life that requires detachment from all relations of proximity. It is a way of life notable for its inability to convert space into time by "making a mark" on it. The individual thus enjoys no relationship with the humans or nature in his immediate vicinity. The nomadic being is a far-off being, a being that belongs to the space between him and the world, which makes distancing into a mode of being. He is a being that believes it is possible to replace closeness in spatial terms (all approach and contact) with temporal proximity, which consists of immediate, albeit quasi-immaterial, availability (*sans* physical presence or contiguity).

It goes without saying that the more the neo-liberal system seeks to collapse the poles of social immobility (the traditional workplace, place of relaxation, or even the family unit); the more it tries to suppress *being* in favor of *becoming*, of the mobile, of the transitory, of a general promotion of the fluid and the flexible over the stable and the connected; the more it does all this, the more people (themselves caught up in a dizzying tornado of transportation, connections, of information coming from all directions and going nowhere, of a system whose parts are infinitely interchangeable yet whose whole is unassimilable, of an existence seemingly outside time, space, and free of context) will become programmed vagabonds, internet itinerants. Wandering is becoming the rule, attachment to place the exception. The new generation of motels will no longer be confined to the periphery of American cities; they will become the new shared horizon of modern life. They will be known under different names: arrivals areas in stations and airports, hotel rooms, metro stations; but the same feeling of alienation will gradually overcome those trapped in these orbits of incessant transit.

Whereas the merchant middle classes from the late Middle Ages down to the middle of the twentieth century made the city into a center of production and exchange, the capitalists of the third industrial revolution demand that the city be a place where it is easy to connect and communicate across large distances. There is no point in deploring this fact. In the name of what would we do so? The organic city of the Middle Ages, governed by a logic of proximity to centers of temporal and religious power? Nevertheless, it is worth pointing out that the present trend is towards urban self-erasure; the city, understood as a centered and quasi-permanent entity, is wiping itself out. At present, even the age of dwelling seems outmoded.

The organization of life (working hours, commuting, leisure, rest) is gradually being decoupled from the organization of space. The diffuseness of inhabited areas, which thanks to new technologies are becoming further and further removed from the heart of the city and are spreading to areas whose connective infrastructure is under development, is leading to the ultimate form of delocalization: the elimination of home-dwelling. The modification of work, from a process designed to transform raw materials into one of information-processing, renders this constant spatial expansion even easier, since the centers of meaning-production are becoming absolutely independent from the actual contours of the terrain. If, as Melvin Weber has argued, "cities develop *only* because proximity means lower transportation and communication costs for those interdependent specialists who must interact with each other frequently or intensively,"[13] it is probable that the ultimate cost reduction will be the abandonment of any ambition of house ownership since any benefit would be nullified by the costs of transport and permanent communication entailed by the necessity of these interactions.

What an impression of the strangeness and obsolescence of the city one gets when one first encounters Los Angeles, a city devoid of urbanity and urban planning, where one can drive for hours without being able to establish whether one has left the city or not, without observing the smallest tangible sign that would indicate a way out; a city that illustrates more starkly than any the way cities have been pulverized into neighborhoods that extend endlessly into the distance, each one impinging upon the next, all of them shrouded in that great leveler and destroyer of distinctions: smog. It would be a mistake to imagine, however, that this space is actually infinite. Better to say limitless in that it draws its existence from the limit and exists solely by virtue of the limit. It also has frontiers, but invisible ones only known to the regular visitor who can recommend one block, but will advise you against walking down another. But in each case, the only means of belonging in this ill-defined and shifting landscape is the car, which traces lines, segments, routes, and curves across space. Walking in this city is considered an indicator of indecency or madness. Only the homeless, dealers of various stripes, and prostitutes still walk around. Outside, everyone moves around from car to car; inside, on escalators and in elevators; but the pedestrian is everywhere in the minority. In actuality, walking isolates the individual, not from contact with her environment (since the American sidewalk is not made for walking on, but is designed to divide one space from another), but rather from other walkers. It may seem paradoxical, but social intimacy is here seen in terms of the car, not in terms of an accidental encounter on the sidewalk. It is thus by dint of its solitary nature and lack of connection to the rest of the community that walking is seen as an improper activity. It is all at once a waste of time and a pursuit unsuited to the essentially infinite environment of the city. That is why the walker immediately stands out as maladjusted (What is he doing?), like a pedestrian on the median divider of a freeway.

The automobile is thus not preferred simply because of its speed (the traffic jams take care of that), but rather because it is perfectly fitted to the city that has been designed to accommodate it. In a strange twist, thanks to the Walkman and rollerblades, the pedestrian is herself turning into a vehicle, shut up inside herself and moving obliviously from place to place. Los Angeles, with its infinite, disorienting space, has invented the social category of urban nomad, the mechanized wanderer who cannot bear to stay at home. In a city where the very notion of a center is anathema, people speed about on virtually infinite ribbons of blacktop, which bear a passing resemblance to the millions of reels of film produced in the nearby studios and spooled on endlessly revolving projector rotors.

Quasi-abstract revelations of this urban dissolution, the most recent paintings by Edward Ruscha (*Chandler-Magnolia*, *Melrose and Orange*, etc.) represent Los Angeles by means of a few intersecting lines on a grey background, whose only embellishments are the names that just about identify them. No particular point of interest is visible beyond the extended grid of all the straight lines intersecting at right angles on monochrome backgrounds, which emerge as if through the afternoon smog. Sometimes, as in *City Grid #2,* a grille of varying density formed by the streets is set in a colored background that recalls the sunlight coming through the windows and illuminating the walls of the room, like a sort of imaginary breathing taking place there amidst the intersections and the city's arteries. But the contrast of colors is a reminder that the true substance (*what is below*) of the city is neither imagination nor air, but its traffic and flatness, those lifelines that are the only things visible at night. The city thus is reduced to its name, its lines, and its map; to its *more geometrico* method for establishing where things belong and how things are to move around, the source of the city's sites and rites. A city disincarnate, she has deigned to become an abstract idea, a concept, in order to come alive again.

NOTES

1 F. L. Wright, *The Living City* (New York: Horizon Press, 1958) 62.
2 Unlike the farm or the village, the big city, it is true, invents itself from whole cloth and owes nothing in terms of its structures to the land on which it lies, but it still depends on its location. For its part, the limitless city is only conceivable in term of movement.
3 Stanley Cavell, *The Senses of Walden* (San Francisco: North Point Press, 1981) 137: "But it is our poverty not to be final but always to be leaving (abandoning whatever we have and have known): to be initial, medial, American."
4 Cavell 138.
5 Henry David Thoreau, *Walden: or Life in the Woods and Other Writings* (Westminster, MD: Modern Library, 2000) 54.
6 Thoreau 54.
7 Thoreau 44.
8 Ralph Waldo Emerson, *Selected Writings of Ralph Waldo Emerson* (Westminster, MD: Modern Library, 2000) 55.
9 Thoreau 681–682.
10 Emerson 55. "The main enterprise of the world for splendor, for extent, is the upbuilding of a man."
11 Cavell 130.

12 Reyner Banham, *Los Angeles: The Architecture of Four Ecologies* (New York: Harper & Row, Publishers, 1971).

13 G. Gerbner, P. Gross, W.R. Melody, eds., *Communications Technology and Social Policy: Understanding The New Cultural Revolution* (New York, NY: Wiley, 1973) 297. The American urban planner Melvin Webber, has authored several important works on the recent changes in the urban environment, including *The Urban Place and the Nonplace Urban Realm, The Post-City Age* (1968), *The Joys of Automobility* (1991), etc.

Translated by Colin Keaveney

MARTHA RONK | from *State of Mind*

Pico Boulevard

From behind the glass they are unmitigatedly still
or passed over. Pico is another.
Driving is to driving as from one end to the other
over bridge and vale. Their eyes unnervingly swerved.
Celan says *over wine and lostness, over*
the running out of both.
I don't find you behind any eyes you open.
After the earthquake it was closed to traffic.
I look at the eyes, the sex, the eyes.
We lap at it fearful of running out,
gulps of red wine. He says
what can the translator mean by *over*?

Neutra's Window

Behind the glass barrier by moving her lips
a woman forms exhortations. Her mind is made up.
What shadows of silence under eucalyptus
where the absence of mirrors protects children
and breaks relentless cycles of words.
Fingers over lips in early portraits marks the mastery
of silent reading, a conclusion of mouth begun by all
who suck out conclusion from the ragged spill
of palm and incumbent dust. The child reads her mind.
Silently and with the stealth of figures pilfered from story
one escapes dominion.

Driving

The film breaks into dialogue after long stretches
of the sort of silence associated with wet roads
and the sounds of tires hissing in the trees as
the wind's an artificial product of moving toward the horizon
as enclosure's only a category of mind.
And then the final exchanges about the weather first
and tentative efforts to snare the other's litany of complaints
the very act of driving was designed to eliminate any sense of.

The Moon over L.A.

The moon moreover spills onto
the paving stone once under foot.
Plants it there one in front.
She is no more than any other except her shoulders forever.
Pull over and give us a kiss.
When it hands over the interchange
she and she and she. A monument to going nowhere,
a piece of work unmade by man. O moon,
rise up and give us ourselves awash and weary –
we've seen it all and don't mind.

DONALD J. WALDIE | *Beautiful and Terrible: Los Angeles and The Image of Suburbia*

We are all citizens of Los Angeles because we have seen so many movies. In the movies, the unquiet image of Los Angeles[1] morphs from city to city: cities of brilliance and cities of *noir*, of structured grids and formless sprawl. The city is revealed as an unsettling place, most often rectified, even by those who live there, by rejecting it. Seen from the shadows of a black-and-white film or imprisoned in the glare of its celebrity culture, Los Angeles looks like a collection of absences: the absence of hierarchies, of serious architecture, of urban intensity, of a center, of authenticity, and often, just the absence of New York. Finally, we are absent from the city, too, wrapped in our own reveries of another Los Angeles that is more adequate to the demands of desire. As Norman Klein has made clear, projecting our own absence onto the blank and indifferent landscape of the city necessarily makes Los Angeles a place of substitution and forgetting.[2] Klein calls this problem "erasure" and he locates it within a larger critique of modernism in its relation to the subordination, displacement, and substitution of memories.

Of course, more is at stake in looking at Los Angeles than a critique of representation. Memory, after all, forms the basis of public policy. Erasure and amnesia were – and continue to be – preconditions for the past fifty years of failed policies for immigrants, commuters, the homeless, homeowners, business operators, and taxpayers. I have the impression that the disturbing qualities of life in Los Angeles that most commentators remark on – and the tendency of Los Angeles to self-immolate in civil discord – reflect a tragic failure of memory. Memory insistently reminds us that contingencies dominate the experience of our lives, that time's arrow will not be stayed, and that authority seeks always to substitute official recollections for those we have labored to hold on to.

In my work as a writer and as a city official, I struggle with questions of memory and its uses: who and what is to be remembered? By what means? From what perspective? And in the condition of being modern – which once made so many assertions about authority to memory – what legitimizing claims can everyday memory assert?

I'm drawn to these questions as they apply to Los Angeles because of what happened when William A. Garnett, in a single-engine Cessna, began in 1950 to fly over six square miles of former lima bean and sugar beet fields about twenty-three miles southeast of the center of Los Angeles.[3] This is what I think happened, taken from the opening pages of *Holy Land: A Suburban Memoir:*

In 1949, three developers bought 3,500 acres of Southern California farmland. They planned to build something that was not exactly a city.

In 1950, before the work of roughing the foundations and pouring concrete began, the three men hired a young photographer with a single-engine plane to document their achievement from the air.

The photographer flew when the foundations of the first houses were poured. He flew again, when the framing was done and later, when the roofers were nearly finished. He flew over the shell of the shopping center that explains this and many other California suburbs.

The three developers were pleased with the results. The black-and-white photographs show immense abstractions on ground the color of the full moon.

Some of the photographs appeared in *Fortune* and other magazines. The developers bound enlargements in a handsome presentation book. I have several pages from one of the copies.

The photographs celebrate house frames precise as cells in a hive and stucco walls fragile as an unearthed bone. Seen from above, the grid is beautiful and terrible.

Four of the young man's photographs became the definition of this suburb, and then of suburbs generally. The photographs look down before the moving vans arrived, and before you and I learned to play hide-and-seek beneath the poisonous oleander trees.

Architectural critics and urban theorists reprinted the photographs in books with names like *God's Own Junkyard*. Forty years later, the same four photographs still stand for the places in which most of us live.

The photographs were images of the developers' crude pride. They report that the grid, briefly empty of associations, is just a pattern predicting itself. The theorists and critics did not look again, forty years later, to see the intersections or calculate in them the joining of interests, limited but attainable, like the leasing of chain stores in a shopping mall.[4]

When Garnett flew over Lakewood – between 1950 and early 1953 – there was ready made a perspective from which the nondescript house lots of Los Angeles could be viewed as a "no place" – as a hyperspace in Fredric Jameson's terms.[5] Selling Los Angeles into existence required that the city be looked down on. The immensity of the Southern California landscape, its relative sameness, its uncertain character as an authentically American place, and the rapid commodification of its square miles into house lots, made the abstractions of aerial photography both necessary and practical. This mode of depicting Los Angeles as acreage to be sold was an established local industry[6] by 1920. Aerial photography had by then acquired an aesthetic that substitutes pattern for topographic coordination and what William Langeweische terms "brutal honesty"[7] for the complexity of everyday experience on the ground. From the air, Los Angeles has no history, no contour except for coastline and foothills, and no human dimension. When Garnett flew, the placelessness of Los Angeles was already available as a cliché, and he would make the building of Lakewood its blighted emblem: the image of suburbia.

On ground the color of the full moon

From the cockpit of his Cessna, photographer William A. Garnett documented the building of the mass-produced suburban tract of Lakewood between 1950 and 1952.

A bombardier's appraising exactness

Garnett's aerial photographs typically lacked an internal scale of reference, the organizing line of the horizon, and identifiable human figures.

In less than 33 months

Mass production turned out 17,500 houses in less than 33 months between 1950 and 1953. Garnett produced "time lapse" sequences of Lakewood's rapid development (top: February 18, 1952, bottom: early December 1952).

William A. Garnett photos
(Author's collection)

Undecorated sheds

The mass produced houses of mid-twentieth century Los Angeles were virtually free of architecture and unencumbered by memory. Which, nonetheless, did not deter eager buyers from wanting one of these pragmatic solutions to the problem of shelter.

Donald J. Waldie: *Beautiful and Terrible...*   57

Rothschild photos
(Author's collection)

What did being modern mean?

It meant aluminum window screens, stainless steel counter tops, garbage disposals in every kitchen, and the room-sized voids into which a variety of historical furniture styles might be introduced.

William A. Garnett and suburbia

When William A. Garnett flew over Lakewood in 1950, he was 34, a veteran of the Second World War, precisely of the same age and experience as tens of thousands of young men and their wives who would buy the houses Garnett looked down on. He had begun his interest in photography at home in Pasadena, building a darkroom with his brother Bernard and taking an early aerial photograph of his high school campus (published later in the school annual) from a seat in a biplane. He intended to study photography at Art Center School in Los Angeles after graduating from high school, but straitened family circumstances forced him to drop out.[8] To help support his family, he picked up commercial photographic work, including some sports photography. In 1940, he went to work for the Pasadena Police Department where he was in charge of crime-scene and evidence photography. His work there included color photographs of fibers seen through a microscope, the first microscope photographs to be admitted as evidence in a California court.

In 1944, he joined the Army Signal Corps and completed training as a motion-picture cameraman just as World War II ended. When he was discharged, Garnett fortuitously hitched a ride home from camp on an overcrowded USAAF transport. The pilot, Garnett later said, let him take the empty navigator's seat in the cockpit. From there, the unfolding landscape below was a revelation. Garnett decided then to become an aerial photographer. When he returned to Los Angeles, he took flying lessons on the GI Bill and started a one-man aerial photographic business. He bought his first light plane in 1947 while still teaching himself how to photograph from the air.

In early 1950, he was hired to document the building of the planned community of Lakewood Park, about 23 miles from downtown Los Angeles. His work for the Lakewood Park Corporation, among other photographic projects, brought him to the attention of New York magazine editors. In March 1954, *Fortune* published "Over California," a seven-page portfolio of Garnett's work selected and introduced by Walker Evans.[9] In his introduction, Evans emphasized the distinction between Garnett's abstract landscapes (which he described as "hand tooled") and the engineering and military aerial photography with which the magazine's readers might be familiar. Evans framed Garnett's aerial photography as a work of transcendence and detachment. "Over California" (which included one of Garnett's Lakewood photographs) led to a long and successful career as a freelance photographer, educator, and environmental advocate.

Encouraged by Edward Weston, Garnett applied for and received the first of three Guggenheim Fellowships (the first to be given to an aerial photographer) – in 1953, 1956, and 1975. In 1955, Garnett had his first individual show at the George Eastman House in Rochester, and his work was included in the "Family of Man" exhibition at the Museum of Modern Art in New York, curated by Edward Steichen.

Although never officially a staff photographer, Garnett had nine photo essays published in *Life* magazine in 1965, the largest photo essay series in that magazine's history. In 1968, he contributed photographs to Nathaniel Owings' *The American Aesthetic*, an influential critique of mid-twentieth century urban planning.

In all his projects, Garnett flew alone, piloting and photographing from the cockpit. He experimented with different camera mounts (including a port in the cockpit floor beneath his feet) and with different camera equipment (including large format cameras). He ultimately settled on two 35mm cameras (one loaded with black-and-white and the other with color film). This combination offered speed and precision, just as his light plane did.

In 1968, Garnett became chairman of the Department of Design at the University of California Berkeley, where he taught photography until he retired as professor emeritus in 1984. He also taught at the Massachusetts Institute of Technology and in workshops with his friend Ansel Adams. Garnett's own books and those (like Owings') that he illustrated, along with his many individual and group shows, his legacy of students, and his participation in the creation and growth of the modern environmental movement, were warmly acknowledged in the news accounts that followed his death in August 2006 at the age of 89.

Garnett's Lakewood photographs – marked by a raking light that poured impenetrable shadows over the flat landscape – were the foundation of an aesthetic that depended for many of its effects on what the photographs typically lacked: an internal scale of reference, the organizing line of the horizon, and identifiable human figures at work. "Garnett's aerial photographs resemble abstract expressionist paintings or views through a microscope," noted the Getty Museum[10] in announcing the museum's acquisition in 2004 of six of Garnett's best-known Lakewood photographs.

But what Garnett saw over Lakewood, however transcending of the earthbound it was, ultimately disheartened him, and he left Los Angeles in 1958. Garnett "didn't like those (Lakewood) photographs so well," his son later told the *Los Angeles Times*. Those photographs – rows of uninhabited houses, treeless streets angling into the frame of the photograph, and interminable workings on featureless ground – lingered in the imagination and merged with newsreel footage of atomic bomb test buildings in the equally featureless Nevada desert. With the publication in 1964 of Peter Blake's *God's Own Junkyard: The Planned Deterioration of America's Landscape*, notes Kazys Varnelis,[11] "the (Lakewood) photographs had become symbols of environmental devastation ... meant to be understood as political avant-garde: both aesthetic and critical." More than symbols, Garnett's Lakewood photographs still serve,[12] more than fifty years after they were taken, as models for how most of Los Angeles is to be remembered – as postcards from suburbia.

With no little irony, images of Lakewood became emblematic of the "no place" of suburbia at the moment when Lakewood no longer was the uncanny place Garnett had photographed only a few months before. By the time one of Garnett's aerial photographs of Lakewood under construction was published in *Fortune*, the landscape of Lakewood had been completely filled in. Between 1950 and late 1952 – in less than 33 months – 17,500 small houses on small lots had been built, sold, and made a home. The process of tract house mass production, which Garnett had documented over Lakewood literally day-by-day, stopped in late 1953 (although it was underway, in slightly altered forms, throughout Los Angeles County). In March 1954, Lakewood had even become a city in the political sense, having completed the first municipal incorporation in California since 1939. The ominously empty city of Garnett's photographs was now crowded with about 100,000 residents.

We can presume that the developers of Lakewood – S. Mark Taper, Ben Weingart, and Louis Boyar – saw Garnett's photographs mostly as a record to be filed with work logs and construction accounts when the project ended.

Ben Weingart, Lakewood developer,
and a William Garnett aerial photomural

"The photographs were images of the developers' crude pride. They report that the grid, briefly empty of associations, is just a pattern predicting itself. The theorists and critics did not look again, forty years later, to see the intersections or calculate in them the joining of interests, limited but attainable, like the leasing of chain stores in a shopping mall." – from *Holy Land: A Suburban Memoir*

Donald J. Waldie: *Beautiful and Terrible...*   63

But I imagine that they looked at some of Garnett's aerial photographs and, because of the kind of men they were, they read into them a grandeur, a collective heroism, of the sort that still clings to the great building projects of the Depression. And we know that Boyer, Taper, and Weingart understood the modernity of their particular act of place making.[13] Indeed, they realized that the Progressive era model of working class housing they had adapted to post-war mass production would result in new relationships to the idea of place. Garnett's oneiric, almost hallucinatory, photographs of deeply shadowed geometric forms on a titanic grid extending, apparently forever, beyond the edge of the image would permanently define that relationship as dread.

Garnett's sumptuous black-and-white photographs were out-of-date as soon as the prints were dry, but the anxieties these photographs evoked about suburban places were timeless. As Scott Beuka has noted,[14] the persistence of anachronistic images of suburbia reveals just how troublesome the suburban landscape of Los Angeles remains. The fixed "symbolic ecology of suburbia" (Albert Hunter) and the "myth of suburbia" (Bennett Berger) are founded, in part, on the continuing shock of seeing Lakewood from the air in 1950 and seeing that its "in between" state could have no relation to the familiar tropes of urban or rural landscapes.

Finding suburbia

Long before Garnet flew over Lakewood, suburban Los Angeles or something very much like it, had been imagined, debated, advocated, and planned for. "Make houses like Fords," department store owner and Progressive activist Edward Filene had insisted in his influential book *The Way Out* in 1925. Make them as cheap and easy to own, too, which ultimately required permanent changes in the national banking system, the invention of entirely new industries, and a reconceptualization of the role of the federal government in housing.

All of which was test marketed everywhere, including in the fox holes of Europe and the jungles of Pacific islands in a series of pamphlets from 1944 and 1945 prepared by the American Historical Association and distributed throughout the theaters of war. When Bill Levitt in 1946, Fritz Burns and Henry J. Kaiser in 1947, and Louis Boyer in 1950 made houses that looked just like those modeled in the wartime pamphlets, the criticism directed at them was that they were "alike as Fords."

A wide-ranging and sophisticated national debate that stretched back to the 1890s, resulting in the creation of a spectacularly successful consumer product, and it looked like Lakewood from the air. I sometimes think the suburbs became the thing labeled "suburbia" because of altitude and broken hearts. Disappointed mid-century modernists and nascent ecologists constructed suburbia from, among other things, some photographs of tract house Los Angeles being built, photographs in which an aesthetic of altitude, a bombardier's appraising exactness, and uncertainty of scale translated immediately into metaphors of ironic distance, a denatured vacuum, and the mechanical replication of enigmas.

What did modernity expect of Lakewood, a housing development that sold itself under the banner "The City of Tomorrow Today"? And what did its residents expect to get out of being modern, other than relief from Depression and the anxiety of the war years? It seemed, at least from the advertising photography commissioned by the developers, that being modern would mean living in a 957-square foot "minimal house" conforming precisely to the model of affordable working class housing that had been imagined from the 1920s on and test marketed during World War II. In deference to Robert Venturi and Denise Scott Brown and their notion of a "decorated shed" – their term for the "ugly and ordinary" in vernacular architecture – the mass produced houses of mid-twentieth century Los Angeles are almost always "undecorated sheds," virtually free of architecture, and unencumbered by any historical memory. Which, nonetheless, did not deter eager buyers from wanting one of these pragmatic solutions to the problem of shelter. Prospective buyers waited in very long lines to buy one. They are not beautiful houses. They are not sentimental. They do not appear to be consoling. It's only their humility that makes them seem ironic.

The photographs in the marketing campaign for Lakewood's "undecorated sheds" offered many images of the modern: aluminum window screens, stainless steel counter tops, garbage disposals in every kitchen, and the room-sized voids into which a variety of historical furniture styles might be introduced. Of course, despite its projection of a hopeful modernity to potential buyers, Lakewood required hardly any selling at all, given the pent up demand for working-class homes in the immediate post-war period. The marketing campaign had a curiously diminished hook: "living." "We're really going to *live* in Lakewood," announced full-page advertisements in the Los Angeles and Long Beach newspapers. Perhaps after having experienced so much disruption in their own lives and having been at least bystanders to so much well-organized death, they did not see the pathos in asserting that just "living" in Lakewood might be a selling point.

What was essentially modern about Lakewood was living within the body of new landscape, on a grid of streets that did not seek to be picturesque or imagine a false pastoral. Lakewood homeowners had to construct "living" from materials handed roughly to them, along with the mortgage papers and a map to the house and lot to which they had been assigned by a salesman who made a $35 commission on every house he sold. What had been marketed naïvely as modern, and had been cast as dystopic even before the moving vans arrived, settled into the commonplace without much regard to the initial sales pitch then or the reductive view of suburbia that came later, in which the post-war, mass-produced tract development was rescripted, in James Howard Kunstler's bleak dismissal, as "the place where evil dwells."

In its representation as suburbia, Los Angeles is preferentially the shrouded city of "treacherous unbrightness," the city that always cheats on its lovers, that is always painted in the colors of smog, the city always seen from a height, from a freeway overpass, from a seat in a descending jetliner, the hapless observer always going under, down to a carcinogenous sea. That imagined Los Angeles continues to be consolation for a certain kind of aesthetic privilege.

William Garnett had recorded a timeless Los Angeles that could be endlessly retrojected back into history as a landscape of loss. Its emblem, of Lakewood seen from the air, remains beautiful and terrible.

NOTES

1 This essay was originally presented as an illustrated survey of photographs of Lakewood (a Los Angeles suburb) taken between 1950 and 1953 by commercial photographers employed by the Lakewood Park Corporation to document the mass-produced housing project the corporation built between 1949 and 1953. Among the photographers who documented the building of Lakewood was William A. Garnett.

2 Norman Klein, *The History of Forgetting: Los Angeles and the Erasure of Memory* (London and New York: Verso, 1997).

3 The photographs that illustrate this essay are from the author's collection or are reprinted with the permission of the City of Lakewood.

4 D.J. Waldie, *Holy Land: A Suburban Memoir* (New York: Norton, 2005).

5 Fredric Jameson, *Postmodernism, or the Cultural Logic of Late Capitalism* (Durham, NC: Duke, 1999).

6 By the end of the First World War, French military reconnaissance units were taking as many as 10,000 aerial photographs a day.

7 William Langeweische, *Inside the Sky* (New York: Vintage, 1999).

8 Jon Thurber, "William Garnett, 89; Took Aerial Photography to Artistic Heights," *Los Angeles Times* 5 Sept. 2006.

9 Walker Evans and William A. Garnett. "Over California," *Fortune* March 1954.

10 "William A. Garnett," *The Getty Museum* 18 Sept. 2006 <www.getty.edu/art/gettyguide>.

11 Kazys Varnelis, "Psychogeography and the End of Planning – Reyner Banham's

Los Angeles: The Architecture of Four Ecologies," *Pop Culture And Postwar American Taste (New Interventions in Art History)*, ed. Patricia Mortin (Oxford: Blackwell, 2006).

12 Most recently they were included in an exhibition at the San Jose Museum of Art "Suburban Escape: The Art of California Sprawl" that also includes photographs by later New Topologists.

13 Interviews of S. Mark Taper conducted by the author.

14 Scott Beuka, *SuburbiaNation: Reading Suburban Landscape in Twentieth-Century American Fiction and Film* (New York: Palgrave, 2004).

NORMAN KLEIN | *Less Is A Trifle More:*
Building A Shaky Future in 2006

Let us imagine that the Enlightenment tradition ended, in stages, after 1989, along with postmodernism, along with pay telephones and independent bookstores. What does that erosion suggest as cultural history – in Los Angeles, and in what we call "Western" civilization, essentially Western Europe and the Americas? First, I must briefly present how this grand erasure took place, and then, imagine what construction – what believable story – museums and historians are conjuring up to take its place.

But we cannot manage that if I do not clear the air of all canonical theory, as practiced from 1960 to 1989. It was a grand moment for critical theory, but now we must rely on it purely as a series of permissions.

Nor should we assume that globalized terminology is the next step in a chain. It is fair to say that the eras since 1989 should not simply be called "globalization." That would be like calling 2006 "all things more or less everywhere." And yet, culturally speaking, we are much closer to that kind of vanishing point, to the end of a vertical order. As of 1989, we were still much farther away. Across the arts, globalized distribution was only partial. Remnants of the old vertical system of culture in Europe and the U.S. were still tottering in place. Distribution was not completely dominated by home entertainment and themed environments. Nor were alternative art markets quite as localized as they are today, underneath the blizzard.

Back in 1989, the "urban metropolis" model of recognition was fading, but still in place, for literature, theater, cinema, even electronic media. By that system, like the Paris Salons of the nineteenth

69

century, each year, or every few years, cultural heroes were anointed, almost officially. A system of juries, mostly through print, decided which writers "must" be read internationally, which artists were transforming visual codes. Perhaps five cities in the U.S. and Europe – and then also Tokyo by 1989 – took on this chore, through journals, awards, mass publishing, museums. They reshuffled the canon authoritatively, with mixed results.

Even poststructuralism, the warning that these canons were rotten, became itself a canon, assigned for classrooms across academia. Similarly, conceptual art went quickly from subversive in 1968 to mainstream. The rhizomatic, the floating, were studied as a new form of order. French theory in translation became a latinate, a catholicity, that explained why latinates were no longer working.

Indeed, precisely when the older cosmopolitan system was crashing, just when help was needed, the hierarchical, cautious streak in universities grew fiercer. In fact, what we call globalization has proven quite conservative across the culture, particularly in universities, in museum curating, in talk radio, in chain bookstores, in national politics.

Between gulps of latte, in fancy new museum eateries, globalized distributors dole out culture in a mulish, cautious way. We can argue that iPods and blogs and wikis – folksonomies – will correct all that. And I will never argue that it will not. One has to leave room for hope. I simply am not all that convinced, particularly for book culture.

So, like a science-fiction novel about a purple cloud dissolving consciousness, we imagine a breach that shook loose the foundations, erased the Enlightenment, more or less in the summer of 1989, exactly two hundred years after the French Revolution. With the help of eye-popping computer graphics, we see the cloud spread. After it strikes, culture begins to resemble a lapse in collective memory, the hundred and first year of solitude. As home entertainment replaces public culture, we enter a kind of aporia. No pain, no blame. We are driving while medicated. We keep trying to find a sign behind the tree, for at least the name of the road we are on.

Let me narrow this aporia to Los Angeles, then broaden it afterward. Los Angeles is often called a place that never quite begins, but never stops, an epic aporia. As I often say, Los Angeles is the city of the future fifteen years too late. But it is also a vital cultural laboratory for ethnic and cultural forms.

In the meantime, no obvious political points should be argued, as if we didn't know. No need to preach to the choir. We all know that global media is a ruthless heresiarch, as Borges might have put it. And I will resist complaining about the monstrous bad faith of the Bush Administration, much as I love to do it. I'll say only that a hundred years from now, kids will dress as Americans for Halloween.

In the 1980s, ending perhaps in 1992, the "L.A. School" was identified, from architects like Gehry, Mayne and even Jerde, to cultural critics like Edward Soja, later Mike Davis. From new studies in geography to labor history, histories of urban planning, malls and shopping, Chicano and black studies, revisionary looks at the police, at real-estate policies, L.A. was revealed as a city caught between branding and investments, a dialectic confusion. Clearly here was the "postmodern city" as of 1890 turning into the industrial city of 1945; and now? Now it was almost unnamable, as the waves of immigration promised to restructure it for the next forty years.

Kevin Starr was underway with his master chronologue on the state of California (now fourteen volumes). The interest in redefining L.A. as an ethnographic "new byzantium" was particularly clear after the success of the 1984 Olympics, despite the ominous changes in policing, that aggravated the growth in street violence after 1984 – and then attempts to ignore what was plainly there.

The museum culture expanded considerably, from the new MOCA to the early Getty institute in Brentwood, to dozens of new galleries, new collectors from the film and TV industries, and the wave of interest – through New York (Metro Gallery, etc.) – in L.A.-trained conceptual artists and painters (many of them linked with John Baldessari, perhaps the key figure, among others identified with Cal Arts).

There was even a trickle of grant money available. In 1985–6, I shared a grant to set up a long lecture series entitled "L.A.: Beneath the Myths," through Beyond Baroque, in the margins of alternative small-press literature, always strong and always ignored, under the shadow of the entertainment economy.

A new visual record appeared on television. In 1986 to 1990, KCET, somewhat cautiously, set up a series of half-hour documentaries on Los Angeles. New public TV series on L.A. politics appeared as well. Then in 1996, Eckhart Schmidt began a pioneering series of German documentaries on L.A., over twenty and more to come, perhaps the largest archive of interviews we have for the past decade.

But the key moment for the imaginary of "globalization" begins after 1981. The vast eighties revival of noir, often by way of science fiction (cyberpunk), brought the public to many forgotten crime writers associated with Los Angeles (notably Jim Thompson, an author reprinted through Black Lizard Press in Berkeley).

An alternative mythic L.A. was practically invented from 1982 to 1992, particularly with the cult fascination of *Blade Runner*, and the posthumous notoriety of Philip K. Dick. If I were imagining this alternative-reality L.A. – how it came to be seen, through film, literature and architecture – I would call it the future as a reenactment of the collapse of industrial capitalism. Like a double-baked potato, the city undergoes another rise and fall similar to the shock of what was called "de-industrialization." That is, by 2019, slums will be reinvented in American cities dominated by Asian influence. Instead of a drug culture, it would be a culture where data is a drug.

Climate would be inverted, floods and droughts changing places. And capitalism would return to a crudeness like the 1840s, or like the Great Depression. Collective memory would vanish. Anarchy would be let loose. The center would not hold.

The L.A. Uprising of 1992 gave a new set of grisly images to go with this alternative story of Los Angeles. The emblematics of globalization began, the eschatological countdown to the end. We already knew that it would look like buildings on fire, even in movie series like *Die Hard* or the *Terminator*; and finally with aliens blowing up buildings in *Mars Attacks* and *Independence Day*. Little did we know how much the meltdown of buildings would become the icon of the new age.

But at the same time, the suburbs matured as the new model for all urban life, even for the design and rhythm of downtowns. Here too, the Los Angeles school, the L.A. experience became paradigmatic. Great L.A. was a congeries of almost forty towns buzzing around and inside the original L.A. (mostly a river city not much larger than San Francisco). Here was a profoundly interiorized belt of hundreds of neighborhoods, where private entertainment far exceeded public life. There was night life, but in many ways, Los Angeles pioneered urban complexity based on home entertainment – particularly in this era from 1982 to 1992, when the new technologies, and the new social and economic arrangements that we call globalization began to restructure cities rapidly.

And then the entire Soviet system collapsed, like dust in the rain. That prompted the NATO alliance, which also included entertainment, to launch into new markets globally. At the same time, the counterpoint to globalization – the new Asia, originally called the five tigers in East Asia – systematically emerged, around China, while Japan recovered from the shocks of the nineties. (I say counterpoint, as in dialectic, because increasingly I see us in a Marxist moment in a "post" Marxist era.) But with business day beginning to rise in the east, suddenly L.A. was called the eastern capital of the Pacific, as L.A.'s expanding port and global trade outpaced all other industries.

Now we pause for a moment, return to the opening statement. Why should a process like the one introduced about L.A. from 1981 into the nineties remove "the Enlightenment tradition." Allow me to answer as my research has shown me: in 1992, I signed a book contract to write a history of simulation, from 1550 to the present. I interrupted work on it to write a history of forgetting, and a giant database novel entitled *Bleeding Through*. But the problem associated with a history of simulated environments only grew. I could not begin with the Renaissance, navigate through the Enlightenment, and wind up with Disneyland, much less with the post 1989 world.

I needed a different point of departure, a different point of origin. History may simply be a box of evidence, with a small engine inside, perhaps not always timeless so much as always about the present; but it still is a profound discipline. It must ply beneath layers, locate the tangible. Of course, the evidence keeps shifting as the need for new points of origin emerge.

And my evidence pointed increasingly toward 1580 and the Baroque as the origins of what led to Disneyland. It was not simply the Enlightenment, but an alternative enlightenment, filled with occult museum toys and painted domed ceilings and optical illusion, and late feudal remnants ready to collapse. In this counter-enlightenment, democracy does not win; nation states do not inevitably get larger; religious fundamentalism is not eradicated. Instead, a fanatical blend of new technology and atavistic madness sets in.

That sounded closer to the spirit of "post" Disneyland, and post-1989. In my last book, on *Freud in Coney Island,* I call this a horizontalizing process, where no vertical urban center can compete as easily as global home entertainment.

In work I plan next – after a large data novel on how the twentieth century was imagined before it was invented – I want to revisit that period 1981 to 1992, to find more cultural roots to our predicament, or rather predicaments. Clearly, Los Angeles is at the heart of this process. And I sense that 1981 fits a new cultural history that is getting trendy anyway.

At the Getty Research Institute and now at the Pompidou Center in Paris, a flurry of shows and acquisitions point toward this new point of origin (as does a new study by Cecile Whiting, on L.A. Pop). We re-imagine the past that leads to the present, as both historians and writers of science fiction. The future begins in the mid-fifties (in *The Vatican to Vegas*, that history of simulation, I call it the Electronic Baroque). Thus, Pop in the U.S., in Germany, in England is the foundation of a culture where simulation and home entertainment compete with public life. It is a kind of nano-journey, where transistors from the sixties point toward GPS computer implants in the nineties, and infinitely less as slightly more in our future.

If the industrial world that we now worship as if it were Pompeii was dominated by the massive – skyscrapers, giant nation states, world wars – our future will exist in layers beneath and inside the radar. It is a granulated, optically scanned future, where many of the working principles of the Enlightenment, and of the urban-centered, vertical civilization will have increasingly less place.

We cannot tell if this is a telescope or microscope, because all data is micronic, but all-powerful. We are asked to wait for painful silences that rumble as loudly as tanks once did. We also see a devolution of the human condition everywhere, signs of slippage.

And yet, the services become more global, the communications grow, even while surveillance and the inability to make political changes seems oddly more difficult. But most of all, we will be asked to live increasingly below this radar, below this data flow. As the political assumptions and cultural modeling that emerged in the nineteenth and twentieth centuries dissolves, we may have to do with much less. The only way to have less and feel as if you have slightly more, is to rely on home entertainment, and cheap data. As our public options slip away, our cell phones improve.

I only hope that this new historical model, from Pop to 2006, where the 1980s becomes the cauldron, along with the 1950s, will take us to a greater humanism. I am old-fashioned enough to still believe in the popular will, and collective democracy, and refuse to sponsor alienation. We may be a mess, but that is what makes the human species unique, that we constantly operate based on our imperfections.

I'll conclude with a kind of liturgical question, because my work on all this is ongoing, and the evidence keeps pouring in: whatever the United States has failed to be, it remains to many the beacon of the Enlightenment. Into a trackless wilderness, the refuse of the human race have been brought. It is a bizarre, even perverse success, but the imaginary of it represents the Enlightenment to many in the world.

Perhaps we have made a mistake relying on the U.S. as this "beacon," this frontier fantasy. But if, in the globalized erosion of the Enlightenment political and cultural traditions (for better as well as worse), this "beacon" finally becomes too ridiculous for even the collective imaginary, then what? When will the human race invent another America, imaginary or otherwise – ruthlessly empty out two continents, and fill them with the marginal and forgotten?

I am studying the future of cities as suburbanized urbanism takes over, and as the public sector vanishes into a kind of urban feudalism in many cities. I watch the shift in global capital, as we all do. I watch the cross-coding of home entertainment with older forms (literature, theater, music, cinema, architecture). I try to learn to see less in order to map the nano logic that is coming so quickly. I am convinced that it is a great opportunity for new cultural forms. I will not be intimidated, nor medicated by it. But I have not a shred of heroism in my nature. I am very much an imperfect man, who wants a level playing field in a horizontal world that is culturally shutting down in many areas. I have no moral high ground either. I feel as corrupted by it as anyone else. And like everyone else, I cannot decide whether I want to be left alone or noticed.

As this cool, polished future of forgetting takes over, we will probably turn increasingly toward very localized forms, to feel intact. As vertical systems corrode, as oversight becomes impossible, the local may be the best form of the global. Perhaps culture in a hundred thousand places that barely notice each other is an answer, not a problem.

What frightens me most is culture of zero tolerance. That means those who have no power are not allowed to be treated with humanity. And those who control have no one overseeing what they do. Hidden inside all the horizontal blogo-phantasms may be a new form of granular dictatorship, a feudal anarchy. Writers and art makers should resist that. If there is a Jefferson reading this paper, please take note.

JEAN-MICHEL ESPITALLIER | *MiscelLAnea*

In Los Angeles the International Airport is called LAX, a code name given by the International Civil Aviation organization, and as the story takes place in Los Angeles, this onomastic degree zero is immediately transcended into a mythological toponym. The stroke of genius is that there is no genius; what is original is this originalness without originality.

In Los Angeles, at the ends of the runways of the international airport, a whole neighborhood was razed to the ground, leaving only lines of asphalt streets which are still visible in this stretch of wasteland overgrown by kerosene-saturated grass.

Action! From the airport, take Sepulveda south. Cross Manchester, then turn right on 83ʳᵈ. Airlane is the sixth street on your left. The Bennett's house is on your immediate right, you'll see an aluminum Airstream, which is always parked a few feet away.

In Los Angeles, it is currently illegal to climb the 45-foot-tall letters of the Hollywood Sign, which was erected in 1923 by real estate agents atop Mount Peel, because fallen and/or attention-starved actors have committed suicide by leaping off this magic word.

In Los Angeles, along Sunset Boulevard, vendors sit at little tables displaying signs that read "Star Maps." Seeing them, a Vietnamese student who had come to California to study astronomy was heard to exclaim: "What a great country!"

In Los Angeles, Arnold Schoenberg trained musicians working in Hollywood studios to compose music for horror movies.

In Los Angeles (in the sky): airliners at high altitude, LAPD helicopters, private helicopters, sightseeing planes, fighter planes on test flights, military planes on manœuvers, cargo planes taking off toward the Pacific, jumbo jets swooping down single file on LAX. Birds adapted to the latitude and climate. Telephone wires dangling from pole to pole, like in westerns. Kites in Redondo Beach. Smoke from El Segundo. Serious pollution (stage 1 alert) every 9 days.

In Los Angeles, one of the biggest treatment plants is called Hyperion.

In Los Angeles, I went with Guy Bennett to Blue Jay Way, a short and winding street in the Hollywood Hills where George Harrison spent a week in August 1967 and where he composed "Blue Jay Way," which came out that December on the *Magical Mystery Tour* album. The fiction of Harrison's song invents the real here, as everywhere else in Los Angeles, where fiction created by Los Angeles generates and regenerates Los Angeles, which is not a fiction but the fiction of a fiction. On Blue Jay Way we came to see that there is nothing to see.

*Action! From Blue Jay Way, turn right on Thrasher and take it to Doheny. Go left on Doheny, cross Sunset, and keep heading south. Turn right on Santa Monica, left on Century Park, then right again on Olympic, which you take all the way to Sepulveda. On Sepulveda turn left, then go straight. Careful: just after Howard Hughes Parkway, you go left on 78*th*; pass Naylor, Truxton, Vicksburg, Croydon, Bleriot, and then turn right – you are on Airlane, the Bennett's house is at the far end on the right, you'll see an aluminum Airstream, which is always parked a few feet away.*

In Los Angeles, just as we do not hear George Harrison's song on Blue Jay Way, we do not see David Lynch's movie on Mulholland Drive.

In Los Angeles, Marina del Rey has the greatest concentration of yachts and sailboats in the world, and Skidrow has the greatest concentration of homeless people in the United States.

Action! From Marina del Rey, take Bora Bora Way, then Via Marina to Washington; turn right. Take Washington to Centinela and take another right. Go down to the Marina Freeway, that you'll take on your left. From there, merge onto the San Diego Freeway and get off on La Tijera. Then turn right on 83rd, Airlane is the second street on your right. The Bennett's house is right there on your right, you'll see an aluminum Airstream, which is always parked a few feet away.

In Los Angeles, the architects of luxurious villas located in chichi Westside neighborhoods and Bel-Air have drawn their inspiration from the high-security construction techniques of military headquarters and American Embassies.

In Los Angeles, large sums of money are spent to fight gangs most of whose members are refugee victims of those Central American totalitarian governments financed by the United States.

In Los Angeles, LAPD helicopters equipped with infrared cameras and high power searchlights patrol the skies over "unsafe" neighborhoods 24 hours a day, finding their way around by the numbers painted on thousands of rooftops which, seen from the sky, give the city the appearance of a game board.

In Los Angeles, LAPD officers call their headquarters "Fort Apache," and use techniques perfected during the Vietnam war when on combing operations in the ghettos.

In Los Angeles, up to the 1980s, the LAPD was known to be more corrupt and more likely to violate the Constitution than any other police force in the country.

In Los Angeles, in the heart of Watts, a new mall – the Martin-Luther-King Center – was proposed to be built on the model of Bentham's Panopticon, with a central control tower, patrols of vigilantes and LAPD officers, outer walls, and video surveillance covering the entire public space.

Action! From Watts, take 103rd Street to Central and turn right. Go to Century and turn left, heading west. Right after the San Diego Freeway, take a right on Aviation, a left on Manchester, then a right on Airport. Go up to 78th and turn left. Airlane is the third street on your left, the Bennett's house is at the end of the street, on the left, you'll see an aluminum Airstream, which is always parked a few feet away.

In Los Angeles, a palimpsest of Japanese-American businesses can be seen on the 1st Street sidewalk in Little Tokyo, where the names of generations of shops located there, both up to and after the expropriation of their owners in the 1940s, have been set into the concrete.

Since 1900, the population of Los Angeles has multiplied by 40 times, that is 105 inhabitants a day, or one every quarter of an hour for more than a century. With 3,696,000 quarter-hours since the 1st of January 1900, when Los Angeles had 100,000 inhabitants, we arrive at the 3,796,000 inhabitants living in Los Angeles today.

In Los Angeles, Angelenos hate to love their city that they love to hate.

In Los Angeles, the R-2508 airspace, which is the biggest military airspace in the world, sees a total of 90,000 sorties every year. With 246 sorties a day, a military plane takes off in R-2508 airspace about every 6 minutes.

Thus we can deduce that each newcomer to Los Angeles causes two military planes to take off in R-2508 airspace.

In Los Angeles, the Big One lies beneath our feet, threatening to return to the desert what was taken from the desert. That's why Los Angeles is a horizontal city, a surface excrescence, with neither depth nor verticality, the city of glide, *slide city*. The constant surfing of cars on the freeways that vein the city, surfing of beach boys on the waters of the Pacific, surfing of the net generation, surfing of approaching jets, the carefree surfing of a carefree "Hollywood" lifestyle. Everything glides in L.A. L.A. glides over everything.

Los Angeles is the city of the future:
– Because on the edges of the city, in the desert, the future settlement of thousands of inhabitants has already been planned, and signs for streets that do not yet exist sketch a blind geography. Toponymy before topography. Location of what will be but does not yet exist. Ghostly traces of the future.
– Because thousands of stars studding the "Walk of Fame" on Hollywood Boulevard are still awaiting names, thus everyone can come dream about the present absence of his or her own name.
– Because Los Angeles is the last city of the American West, and thus in Los Angeles the Orient is west, and the West is the Orient. Now the future of America having always been in the West, and the future of the world today being in the Orient, it ensues that Los Angeles is the city closest to the future.
– Because confronted with the Hollywood machine, Adorno concluded that "In America, one will not be able to dodge the question, whether the term culture, in which one grew up, has become obsolete."
– Because Los Angeles is the only city in the world to be called by its initials, and because "L.A.," which does not mean exactly the same thing as "Los Angeles," is Los Angeles' famous *name*.
– Because in Los Angeles 86 languages are spoken.
– Because in Los Angeles the power is in finance, in media, in Asia, and in the police.
– Because in Los Angeles, the metropole is the most militarized city in the United States.

– Because in Los Angeles, which was the capital of the reign of the automobile, car manufacturers are sued for the role they have played in global warming.
– Because in Los Angeles, the future is the Big One.
And because it has been a long time coming.

Translated by Béatrice Mousli

SOPHIE DANNENMÜLLER | *Made in L.A.*

Art made in Los Angeles can be understood at least in part by looking at the historical period when its defining characteristics appeared, when the sprawling metropolis became "America's second art city," and its provincial art scene burst into national and then international prominence. During the key period of the 1960s, an art infrastructure developed, encouraging new styles and talents. Some of the specificities of the art made in Los Angeles became noticeable: freedom from academicism, desire for innovation, closeness to popular culture, connection to real life, and political engagement. Moreover, the omni-present Los Angeles urban environment itself acted as a filter through which the artists created, constantly renewing their inspiration.

America's Second Art City

In a 1963 article entitled "Los Angeles: America's Second Art City," Jules Langsner wrote:

> In the space of a half-dozen years the status of Los Angeles in the art community has changed from the home of the nuts who diet on nutburgers to a lively and vital center of increasing importance on the international art map, having become in the interim the country's second city with regards to caliber and number of galleries, collectors, museum activities, and creatively prodigal painters, sculptors and printmakers.[1]

Similarly, in a special West Coast issue of *Art in America*, Gifford Philips noticed in 1964 that "California [was] in the midst of a phenomenal art boom."[2] Several factors contributed to the radical transformation of the Los Angeles art scene that took place in the early sixties. Firstly, the economic conditions were favorable. The region's employment rate was good and the L.A. area population soon became second in size to New York. In this prosperous context, regional pride probably contributed to the burgeoning local art scene – Los Angeles refusing to be lagging behind other big cities any more, as it was in the 1950s when it was deemed a "cultural wasteland." Nevertheless, it wasn't the city administration that developed an official program to support the arts, but rather private initiatives that transformed the art scene from within. For example, a new generation of local art critics began to cover Los Angeles and to give visibility to emerging artists in national and international art periodicals. *Art in America*[3] had Billy Al Bengston design a cover, and a *Milk Bottle* by Joe Goode made the cover of *Artforum*[4] only a few months after the publication was launched in San Francisco. In fact, *Artforum*'s move to Los Angeles in 1965 (before settling in New York in 1967) further consolidated the increasing importance of the City of Angels on the art map. In addition, numerous art galleries opened in the early sixties, totaling 70 in 1964. Many of them were clustered on La Cienaga near the legendary Ferus Gallery, co-founded by Walter Hopps and Edward Kienholz in 1957, which was a seminal early influence on the local art scene. In a city without a center and where activities were consequently scattered and difficult to locate, the concentration of galleries in one area attracted attention to the arts. Thus, the "Monday Night Art Walks" – a weekly event during which the La Cienaga galleries stayed open late – became such a great success that a gallery owner complained about his gallery being flooded with over 2,000 people each Monday![5] Naturally the art market flourished and the sales of artworks to local collectors tripled within five years in the early 1960s.[6] The new crop of collectors was adventurous and knowledgeable in contemporary art, due in part to the UCLA Art Department extension classes given by art historians in the art galleries, or at the collectors' homes. As expected, the classes helped develop their taste for contemporary art, and the neophyte collectors also benefited from professional advice from the outset, often buying works by local artists they personally knew. In addition they played a considerable role in the newly established Contemporary Art Council of the LACMA, by supporting the Museum's acquisitions. The art institutions were undergoing change as well. In 1961, the Los Angeles County Museum of Art was created, eventually moving to a building of its own in 1965. Significantly, the LACMA was the largest museum built in the United States since the 1941 National Gallery of Art in Washington, D.C. At the same time, the Pasadena Art Museum was taking a progressive turn under the influence of Thomas Leavitt and Walter Hopps – acquiring contemporary works, and mounting exhibitions of twentieth century art, such as the first Marcel Duchamp retrospective in 1963, and also moving to a modern building in 1969.

Of course, none of this would have been possible without the simultaneous emergence of a cohort of young artists with innovative styles and vanguard talent.

Made in L.A.

A tour of the galleries and artist's studios in the mid 1960s in Los Angeles would have offered a remarkable array of styles and mediums. Since the late 1950s, John McLaughlin, Lorser Feitelson, and others, had perfected a Hard-Edge painting style, which influenced the so-called Finish Fetish style (or L.A. Look). Representative of Finish Fetish would be the sleek and bright sculptures of John McCracken and Craig Kauffman, to name only a couple, that were at times compared to a colorful blend of Minimalism and Pop Art. With a very different aesthetic approach, Gordon Wagner, Edward Kienholz, Wallace Berman, George Herms, and others created assemblages with ordinary and cast-off objects found in the local dumps or thrift shops. L.A.'s own sort of Pop style was also thriving with Ed Ruscha, Joe Goode, David Hockney, and Vija Celmins, among others. Doug Wheeler, James Turell, and Bob Irwin were beginning to form what would be labeled the Light & Space movement by the end of the decade, and Conceptual Art was taking shape – so to speak – in the work of John Baldessari. This small sampling already gives a good idea of the diverse styles, forms and media that comprised Los Angeles art. In consequence, it would be unfair to speak of an intrinsic single aesthetic, school, or style. Although, in examining the stance of the artists or their creative approach, it is possible to discern a few characteristics that help define the art made in L.A. as, all at once, an art of freedom, of experimentation, close to the vernacular, involved with real life, and politically engaged.

Art history, traditions and academicism had little hold on Los Angeles artists who felt free to create as they wished, with an attitude resembling that of the pioneers. After all, California was the last frontier, the edge of the land at the end of the journey, which might prompt a desire to break with the past, do away with traditions and embrace the new. The artists' frame of mind is also suggestive of that of entrepreneurs: looking toward the future, solving problems, obtaining results, and counting only on themselves to carry out their projects, notwithstanding a general public apathy. The painter Lari Pittman summed it up this way: "I think here you can grow like a weed – with sweet neglect. That's really been part of the history of Los Angeles, thriving like a weed. Maybe that indifference actually fuels production to a degree."[7] In other words, the artists felt free to experiment without inhibition since no one seemed to care.

This climate of "sweet neglect" encouraged experimentation with ground-breaking techniques and materials in art making. In fact, the list of techniques and materials in works of art at the time suggests that of the research and development department of some revolutionary enterprise. Traditional mediums like ceramics and photography were completely revisited. Peter Voulkos, Ken Price and John Mason changed the status of ceramic objects, from utilitarian vessels into *bona fide* works of art. Wallace Berman used an outmoded photocopy machine to make his series of *Verifax Collages,* and Robert Heinecken manipulated photos found in magazines – both demonstrating a totally new attitude towards photography, although they didn't use cameras to do so. Other artists didn't hesitate to exploit advanced technology materials, borrowed from local cutting-edge manufacturers: McCracken innovated with fiberglass; Peter Alexander made sculptures with polymer resins; Larry Bell built *Cubes* with glass coated with silicon monoxide and chrome; and the Light & Space artists employed various luminous gases. The close relationship between the fine arts and avant-garde techniques was confirmed with the LACMA's "Art & Technology" program (1969–1971) which paired artists with local corporations willing to offer their technological expertise to realize the artist's project.

However, artists weren't exclusively interested in cutting-edge materials and industrial processes; they were fond of vernacular forms too. So much so that one could speak of a plebeian type of art in Los Angeles, in the sense that it was close to popular culture. In general, the young Angeleno artists didn't make up an elite group above or apart from the rest of the community. Art was a serious matter, but at the same time the artists refused to take themselves too seriously. Like other youths, they enjoyed popular trends and activities as can be seen in several Ferus Gallery exhibition posters showing Billy Al Bengston riding a motorbike or Kenneth Price balancing on a surf board, and in Joe Goode's *1969 calendar of l.a. artists in their cars.* In effect, "fine" artists were influenced by the shapes and colors of surfboards and hotrods, the craftsmanship and ingenuity, and the iconoclastic approach to design of customizers like Von Dutch, George Barris and Ed Roth.

All of this shows how much artists in L.A. were involved with, acted in and responded to the world around them. This is demonstrated in the way they created works that engaged themselves or the viewers in very direct experiences. In a Light & Space environment, for instance, the viewers become physically involved because of the immersion in colored light in a different way than when looking at an autonomous traditional art object. James Turrell, Doug Wheeler or Robert Irwin weren't only shaping light into sculptural works, like a sculptor would a conventional material. They also intended to directly challenge the viewers' sense of perception to make them aware of the very process of perception and at the same time of their physical presence in the world and their relation to the world through their senses. Other artists on the contrary recreated the ordinary to make it noticeable and thus raise the viewers' awareness of it. A case in point would be Kienholz's *Barney's Beanery* (1964) which is a true-to-life replica, in a slightly reduced size, of an existing L.A. artists' hangout. The first time Kienholz exhibited *Barney's Beanery*, he chose to do so in the parking lot of the real place. He thus confronted art and life, the actual bar and its mirror image, blurring the boundary between the two. As with all of Kienhloz' tableaux, the viewers were invited to step into the scene (which replicated sounds and odors as well) just like they walked into The Beanery in real life. One can only imagine how confused visitors might have felt, especially after a few drinks! Patrons could not order real drinks in Kienholz's tavern, but Allen Ruppersberg's *Al's Café* (1969) fused together an art installation and an American diner where people sat at tables and were served drinks and platters – except that the items on the plates were more akin to assemblages or sculptures than to food. It was however with Performance Art in the 1970s that the dilution of art into life or of life into art reached the peak, in particular when artists put themselves physically at risk and challenged their own limits. For example when Chris Burden had himself shot in the arm by a friend in a performance entitled *Shoot* (1971), or had himself crucified onto a car in *Trans-Fixed* (1974). Not as perilous, feminist artist's performances also questioned the role of art in the world, and the connection between art and life, as they meant to overtly expose that the personal is political, as in *Waiting* (1972) by Faith Wilding who passively enumerated all of the instances of waiting in a woman's life.

Political engagement was (and still is) an important component of the art made in California and an essential creative trigger.[8] It is well known that California was the breeding ground for many countercultural and radical groups: Beats and hippies, Free Speech movement, United Farm Workers, anti-Vietnam War protest, Black Panther Party, Brown Berets, Red Power, Feminism, gay liberation, environmental activism. It is therefore not surprising that here more than elsewhere artists expressed, even promoted their political beliefs in their work and resorted to new forms of expression to do so, such as posters and murals. To demonstrate their disagreement with the government's policy in Vietnam, the Artists' Protest Committee, formed by Irving Petlin and others, erected the *Artists' Peace Tower* in 1966 in the heart of Hollywood. Clearly, reaction against the war in Vietnam was particularly strong because of the geographic position of the state and the heavy presence of the defense industry in California. However L.A. artists responded with the same passion to other crucial issues such as racism and discrimination, civil rights, freedom of speech, and community identity. Among other examples, Salvador Roberto Torres' painting *Viva la Raza* (1969) made up a visual Chicano manifesto, while Betye Saar's assemblage *The Liberation of Aunt Jemima* (1972) spoke against racism as much as for women's liberation. The celebrated *The Dinner Party* (1974–79), by a collective of feminist artists led by Judy Chicago, was an attempt to revisit the history of mankind with the inclusion of women. It is important to note that for these different groups and people, art was used as a vehicle to serve a community and its ideals, to convey a political message, and raise public awareness in the hope to transform society.

Looking through the windshield

The omnipresent urban milieu itself was another significant influence on the art made in Los Angeles. It was a main motif for many artists: Hockney, Ruscha, Baldessari and others depicted the city in paintings, in photos or otherwise. In their work, the artists represented and thus shaped a certain image of Los Angeles, which they virtually imposed on the viewers. They seldom chose to show notable old buildings or historical sights, as if the city had no past, as if it all started with their young gaze. So they preferred the swimming pools, the palm tree-lined avenues, the modern style houses, the new buildings, the highways, the colorful trademarks and ads... They focused on the idiosyncrasies of the modern city, exposing its contemporaneity and its reality, its splendor and its misery, its promises and its limitations. They showed the commonplace as well, the banality of the sprawling city, which was indeed such a significant theme for Baldessari that the nondescript practically turned into another distinctive feature of the metropolis in his "photo-texts" of the 1960s. Other artists paid attention to transitory urban areas such as vacant lots, zones under overpasses, abandoned structures, or dumps – where the assemblagists rummaged to find their art material for instance. In 1967, Allen Kaprow staged a happening, *Fluid,* simultaneously in 15 unremarkable places of Los Angeles and its surroundings. In 1972, a group of feminist artists found and appropriated an old abandoned house which they revamped into *Womanhouse,* a venue for installations and performances. As well, artists from the Chicano community took over the bare walls of the barrios to paint murals, which were often collective projects like the *Great Wall of Los Angeles* (1974–1978) directed by Judith Baca. All of these artistic actions had for effect to draw public attention to usually ignored urban areas, and also to point out the needs of underprivileged communities and neglected neighborhoods.[9]

The region changed dramatically in the 1950s and 1960s; tremendous population growth prompted the construction of highways, tract houses, high-rises and other urban structures. In 1967, more than 90% of all California residents lived in urban areas, and 41% lived in the southern part of the state. So California was both the most populated and the most urban state of the Union. No wonder then that nature was hardly present in L.A. art, even though it had fascinated generations of local artists until the 1950s. It is perhaps Llyn Foulkes' paintings that best exemplify the transitional period, the shift from nature to urban landscapes in L.A. art, as in *Junction 395* (1965), where the mountain disappears, from all angles, behind the stripes of road signs that warn of some imminent danger up ahead.

At the same time, artists presented a fragmented view of Los Angeles, certainly as a response to the impossibility of grasping the vastness of the urban sprawl in one glance. Naturally, the car comes to mind as a necessary component to capture the city, and with it, the particular point of view it provides. It is a view framed by the windshield, complete with rear view mirror, wipers, and part of the dashboard, as in Dennis Hopper's *Double Standard* (1961) or Vija Celmins' *Freeway* (1966). The car offers a means to observe the surroundings without hiding and without being really noticed either, an infiltration into the social body to explore its arteries that blurs the boundary between private and public, between intimate and collective, between inside and outside.

Different from walking, this mode of transportation also alters the driver's relation to time, and the attention span given to what is seen. Some things are just noticed in passing, those alongside the road, as in *Every Building on the Sunset Strip* by Ruscha (1966). But mostly the driver carefully watches the road in front, conceivably killing time on the long and unexciting journey, as Baldessari suggested in *The Back of All the Trucks Passed While Driving from Los Angeles to Santa Barbara, Calif. Sunday 20 Jan. 63* (1963). Finally, the stops at gas stations give the driver the opportunity to step out of the car and take a look at the surroundings from a different angle, perhaps as Ruscha did in *Twenty-six Gasoline Stations* (1962).

Many other examples could illustrate that Los Angeles wasn't only a subject to be represented – the case with many other capitals after all – but that it also acted as a filter through which the artists comprehended the world around them. Because of its morphology, its heterogeneity, its mythology, Los Angeles had an impact on the nature of the art, as well as on the artist's work process, creativity and

NOTES

1   Jules Langsner, "Los Angeles: America's Second Art City," *Art in America* 51.2 (April 1963): 127–131.
2   Gifford Philips, "Editorial – Culture on the Coast," *Art in America* 52.3 (June 1964): 22–23.
3   *Art in America* 52.3 (June 1964): cover.
4   *Artforum* 1.6 (November 1962): cover.
5   Langsner.
6   Philips.
7   Lari Pittman quoted in Terry R. Myers, "Art School Rules," *Sunshine and Noir, Art in L.A. 1960–1997* (Humlebaek, Denmark: Louisiana Museum of Modern Art, 1997) 202.
8   For more on this subject see Peter Selz, *Art of Engagement, Visual Politics in California and Beyond* (Berkeley: University of California Press, 2006).
9   For more on this subject see chapter 5 of Cécile Whiting's *Pop L.A.: Art and The City in The 1960s* (Berkeley: University of California Press, 2006).

HAL GLICKSMAN | *A Discussion of Los Angeles Art*

This text is a transcription by Hal Glicksman of the impromptu talk that he gave at the conference. It concludes with his responses to questions from the audience.

I experienced L.A. art from the '50s through the '80s, and what is so amazing is how tiny it was and unsupported it was in the '50s. For instance, Wallace Berman, who is so important now, published 200 copies of *Semina* magazine and gave most of them away, and half of them were to people in San Francisco. At UCLA, which has graduated so many important artists, the inspiration was gallery director Fred Wight. I don't think he showed a single L.A. artist the entire time he was there. He showed art from Europe. The vision of art in Los Angeles was that modern art came from Europe, especially Picasso and the Surrealists. Those were the artists that were collected in L.A. and slides of their work were used as examples in art history classes. The modern art history class never got as far as New York artists.

There was very active hostility, it is hard to believe, toward abstract expressionism. There were two main painting salons every year in L.A. in the '50s. In the County museum, where art mixed with history and dinosaurs, there was a juried exhibition. When the show generated controversy over abstract art for two years in a row, the county supervisors closed the exhibition.

The city had an open, all-city art festival in Barnsdall Park every year. Kienholz got the job of installing the exhibition. He invited Bengston and all his friends from Venice, California to bring work, which was hung outside in the park over a weekend. That was the last time that annual exhibition was held.

The Ferus gallery was a tiny little galley behind a shutter shop. You could not even see it from the street. You had to know it was there.

About 40–50 people showed up for openings, and half the artists that they showed were from San Francisco. I'm amazed now when I go to museums and see so many thousands of people interested in art. I assure you that when the most interesting things were occurring in Los Angeles, the audience for them was absolutely tiny.

When the Los Angeles County Museum moved to its present location, it opened with a show of New York art. When the Pasadena Art Museum opened a new building, they showed New York art. Two years after these museums opened, they each did large group exhibitions of L.A. art relegated to the summer months.

There were wonderful artists living in L.A. in the early 1960s, especially Sam Francis and Richard Diebenkorn, who were an inspiration to younger artists. But both of those artists moved to Los Angeles from San Francisco with their market already established. They didn't dream of living by selling art just to people in Los Angeles. Young artists assumed they would have to get a New York gallery or a teaching job to live. The development of a market lagged way behind the development of the most interesting art. George Herms and the Assemblage artists, those at the beginning of the Pompidou Los Angeles exhibition, sold to friends or gave their work away.

There were counterparts in Los Angeles to what was going on in New York and the rest of the world. For instance Ed Ruscha was solidly part of the milieu of Pop Art. There were also things absolutely unique to Los Angeles. The most important, I think, are the Light and Space artists. This is what I showed. There was nothing else like this anywhere in the world. I am interested in what is unique and wasn't just an L.A. version of what went on other places. The not-so-benign neglect of local artists might have been a factor in the direction L.A. developed. Wallace Berman lived a beautiful life without any money. Wallace could have sold work, but preferred to not make work that was for sale for a certain purity that he believed in for his art. In 1964 he decided that he had to support his family, and started to produce the Verifax collages, but for an important part of his career, 1957–64, he did not produce art for sale. He was an example of the belief that the purest art was outside the art market. Baldessari, in spite of all of his success, originally made art that he thought only other artists would like, sort of Arte Povera/Conceptual Art purity. A belief that if it were for sale it was somehow suspect. This attitude was encouraged, of course, by people who didn't buy his things until the 1980s.

There was an important dialog in the early 1970s between Michael Asher and Daniel Burin about making art for sale. Michael Asher made rooms. He made a wonderful room as part of the "Market Street" program where Robert Irwin let artists make art out of his studio space. There was nothing for sale and the artists invited each other to show in the space. Asher painted three surfaces of the space black: the ceiling, the left wall and the back wall. That was the entire exhibition. Asher was invited to Dokumenta. There he made a room that was divided down the center into black and white. Half of the ceiling, floor and back wall, and the entire left wall were black. The organizers of Dokumenta built a room for Michael to work in. Burin pointed out that the room they built was essentially a large object. If a space-man were looking down at the Earth he would see a little sculpture painted on the inside. It was not Arte Povera because it required, first of all, a museum to give you a space and the patronage of the establishment to build elaborate constructions. Burin was working out in the streets putting things anywhere and everywhere, but not for sale. This dialog continued for several years in the 1970s as both artists showed in the Claire Copley Gallery in Los Angeles.

Burin did a piece where there was nothing in the gallery. The gallery was on a little courtyard, so there was a passage next to the gallery with windows into the gallery that, naturally, got boarded up to create wall space within the gallery to hang artwork. Burin put his stripes on the inside of the gallery corresponding to the positions of the windows on the outside of the walls. On the opposite wall outside the gallery, across from the wall with the windows, Burin put his stripes on a plain concrete-block wall next to a parking lot. The owner of a little dry-cleaning place on this parking lot completely freaked-out that an artist should be pasting stripes on what she considered to be her parking lot wall. She said "There is nothing ever in this gallery. It is completely empty." Michael Asher did the next exhibition, in which he took out the back partition of the gallery, which separated the exhibition space from the office. This was his interpretation of revealing how art worked. The real energy of a gallery is the office space behind the partition. Burin revealed how the space had been closed up but really had little windows, and Asher revealed how it functioned, so they had this dialog back and forth. Michael decided that from then on he would not do any rooms, just create situations that would tell you something about how the art world functioned. For instance, Michael had a show at the Fort Worth Art Museum in Texas that was in a park with two other museums. One showed European masters and the other showed western art: pictures of cowboys on horses. Asher told the employees of these museums to park in each other's parking lots, and this was his work for the exhibition.

I showed many things like that. At the University of California, Irvine I showed Light-Space and conceptual artists one right after another. In 1975, I was invited to go to the Otis Art Institute to run the gallery there. My timing could not have been worse. The Otis Art Institute was part of the Los Angeles County government structure. It was the strangest thing for them to have an art school, but it happened because the owner of the Los Angeles Times gave his estate to the county for an art school. It had a very long history as an art school, but the county had no way of dealing with it as an enterprise or an activity. This is so unlike Europe, where governments sponsor many cultural things. Government is very uncomfortable in the United States sponsoring art. The school had to eliminate county sponsorship or else close. They didn't have a board of directors, the county supervisors ran it, so they took a small group of friends of the arts and formed it into a sort of board to look for sponsorship. Otis eventually merged with Parsons School of Design and later became what they are now, an independent art school. But during this period when the County was looking down their neck, there I was, leaving the gallery essentially empty. The only time a county supervisor ever came to visit, I was having a show by Jane Reynolds.[1] Her work consisted of removing a tile from the galley floor revealing all of the interesting machinery that was underneath the gallery; pipes and air conditioning pumps and steam boilers as a contrast to the purity of the gallery space. But you don't just lift up a tile and reveal what is underneath. There is a concrete floor under there. We had to drill a round hole through the concrete and then cast a square hole to make it look as if a tile were just lifted out. Of course, because it was a county building, I got into incredible trouble for doing that. The only time a supervisor comes and the gallery is empty with a hole through the county's property.

Daniel Burin did an exhibition for me at Otis. The president of the Otis Art Associates, the group responsible for finding new sponsors for Otis, came into the gallery. She took one look at Burin's stripes on the ceiling of the gallery, and reeled back as if she were hit in the face with a wet mop. "This is the reason we are loosing our school." She blamed the whole thing on me.

The Art Associates hated the Richard Tuttle show at Otis in 1976 that originated at the Whitney Museum in New York. It was also the end at the Whitney for the curator of the exhibition, Marsha Tucker. But she started her own museum, so it ended up a good thing. The Whitney gave Tuttle a major retrospective just last year.

The patronage for art was very small in Los Angeles in the '70s and earlier, but just a short time later Art was outdrawing Baseball as an activity. I don't think art is bigger than soccer in Europe, but patronage of art is huge everywhere and people flock to museums.

Another important aspect of L.A. art is a basis in mysticism and meditation. The previous speaker mentioned how many religions there are in L.A.. Every religion in the world (there may be an exception or two) is represented to some extent in L.A. and many have originated in L.A. and spread around the world. There was recently the 100th anniversary of Evangelical Christianity. I just found out it started in Long Beach, a suburb of Los Angeles. The light and space artists had a basis in Zen Buddhism and other mystical practices that went back to the turn of the nineteenth century in California. The Green Brothers and other architects based their work on Japanese temples and Zen gardens. Light and Space art is the one art form completely unique to L.A. It has not been done anywhere else in the world or by any other generation except that of Robert Irwin, James Turrell and Maria Nordman. Those were the artists I was interested in.

In response to a question about the comparison of minimalism in New York and Los Angeles:

Compare the same basic rectangular shape used by John McCracken in L.A. and Robert Morris in New York. The shape is similar but the surface is different. Morris and Don Judd and artists like them come from a conceptual basis. The surface of the work is neutral gray and not in itself interesting. McCracken's work has a sensual colored surface that comes from a perceptual basis for the work; looking at the work for its visual sensations. There is a very interesting evolution of this perceptual approach. Billy Al Bengston is not usually associated with optical or perceptual art; he does very decorative kinds of things. His early work, however, was the basis for Irwin's very clean perceptual paintings. Both artists started with abstract expressionism and Hans Hoffman's concept of "push and pull." This is the phenomenon of certain colors projecting forward and others receding in space. Bengston created juxtapositions of color in his abstract expressionist paintings that would appear to hover and switch between pushing and pulling in space. When he created the rather decorative optical paintings of 1964 that are in the Beaubourg exhibition, the important feature is the hovering of shapes in space that allowed you to look at these painting for a longer time. It was a very simple but interesting device to create a shape with a contrasting colored gradated border that would simulate what happens in your eye when you look at a solid color shape for a long time.

Robert Irwin picked up the problem of how a viewer could gaze at a painting for a very long time and zone out in the process. When you look at something for a long time it disappears. You see vibrating shapes in your eyes and your eyes wander away from what you were looking at. Irwin created his dot paintings of the mid sixties in response to the perceptual phenomena in Bengston's work and in abstract expressionism.

In response to the discussion regarding the difference between New York and Los Angeles art:

The L.A. artists didn't have Clement Greenberg to write about their work, so they didn't have to think about the verbal description of their work. The artists looked at each other's work and gathered information visually. Visual thinking does not use words. There is also the Zen attitude that it cannot be described in words. So there was a dialog: I do a painting, you do a painting, another one does a sculpture, and they work one off another without having been analyzed in terms of words as a necessary step in between. Again that was the perceptual as opposed to the conceptual way of working.

The light-space artists for a long time refused to have their work photographed, so they weren't written about either, adding to the non-verbal dialog.

In response to a discussion about the absence of Chicano art in the Beaubourg exhibition:

This is an interesting story: I had an old Volkswagen bus that couldn't go on the freeway, so I started driving on city streets between Pasadena and Los Angeles. I fell in love with graffiti. I thought that the work was interesting as calligraphy. I'm really sorry that it is now one of America's main exports to France because it has gotten a little out of hand. At the time it was much less of colored bubbles and more about calligraphy. I started photographing graffiti and did an exhibition of it at Pomona College in 1970. At the same time there was a work of light and space art in another room of the gallery. Three years later, when I was at UC Irvine, a graduate student named Gilbert Lujan came to me. He had seen the graffiti exhibition and asked what I would do next with Chicano art. I said I was not from that culture, so I did not have access to much of it, but I liked the few glimpses I had of hubcaps and car parts used as decorations in peoples homes. He asked if I was interested in altars that people built. I said I had no way of getting to see any.

The faculty at Irvine produced very formal abstract art. Lujan created a sculpture that on one side was a Don Judd pure cube in red painted sheet metal. On the other side was the shape of a stylized dog. The sculpture morphed from Don Judd to Chicano dog. It was very witty and sophisticated. I asked him to put together a list of artists, and we came up with the idea for Los Four: Carlos Almaraz, Robert de La Rocha, Gilbert Lujan and Frank Romero. I was very disturbed by the success of Los Four because I felt as if I had unleashed a movement. I did not want to start an art movement or have anything to do with a movement because there was then pressure on all young artists from that culture to create Chicano art. I showed individual Chicano artists after that, but never as a group. I have since changed my mind about Chicano art. It has matured and moved to a second generation. There is a real beauty and honesty to the Day of the Dead celebrations and the work of groups like Self-Help Graphics in East Los Angeles.

I wanted to make the point that Charles Almaraz started his career as a formal, hard-edge painter with an exhibition at Park Place Gallery in New York. Frank Romero worked for Deborah Sussman who designed the graphics for the Los Angeles Olympic Games in 1984. He was trained by Charles Eames and designed museum catalogs in pure International style. After being formally trained and working as sophisticated artists, they returned to their culture for sources for their art. The same thing is true of the great Mexican painter Diego Rivera. He went to Paris to learn art and painted cubist paintings.

He went back to Mexico with the knowledge and sophistication of modern art in order to find an authentic source and iconography within his own Mexican culture. Viewers looking at Chicano art don't see that is has a basis in sophistication rather than naivety.

In response to a question about the current developments in L.A. art.

New York artist Ad Reinhardt had a monthly page in *Art News* in the 1950s and early '60s of diagrams and collages explaining theories of contemporary art. A famous one of these showed modern art as a tree with movements as branches and artists as leaves. But it was a tree with the newest thing growing out of the top. The concept that art had a mainstream, and that art was going somewhere, ended in the 1980s. I like to think of art now as a shrub, completely rounded, with everything growing outward with no peak or direction. It is a fascinating contrast to the '60s where one thing was brand new and nothing earlier was important after that.

NOTES

1   The exhibition was *Alice Aycock And Jane Reynolds,* October 13–November 21, 1976.

© RMcN

PAUL VANGELISTI | *from "Alabaster"*

Voluntary

About blessings parenthetical screaming in the mud.
Baseball absolutely demands if not sanctifies the wait.
Cover both, my love, with the lull of our tender drifting.
Doubt claims eternity not the bushtits fussy squeaking.
Each day redeems the leaky song of presiding clichés.
From every device only alibis remember to ring.
Green fire under the mountaintops, armor not your heart.
Hi-ya-yaya, going going gone the corazon of
inaction. Hark, hark, it's not just dogs howling at shadows.
Jericho, in any case, is projected just east of downtown.
Keeping jargon in charge slightly lessens the sway of hips.
Lingering knowledge of what, she demands, terse genuflection?
Mild low pressure and light winds find June softly eternal.
No more what, he thinks, birdsong floating black cat's sleepy form
or now two butterflies chasing among half-lit guava.
Peculiar options resist something less than bucolic or
quintessentially parochial in weighing Sunday
reasons, quite apart from chance, for the adventure of
surviving rightly or wrongly a most outlandish romance.
There, said it all, he thought, warblers out-mewling the dogs.
Unless echoes count, the passing as well as the coming.
Victory upends the arrogant poverty of your claim.
With vague lessons of trust, emptiness as a way of singing.
Expect what you will, each hill feels like a pleasure taken.
Yet, exactly now, still minding a chalice in that last chance.
Zip, zap, longing is no better sometimes than lying.

Wafer

Alternating blessedly the cosmos inside and out,
beyond any glint of remorse in a company town
casually born of cynicism kneeling in the sun.
Daddy calls to say that lions are infiltrating your chance,
early data might indicate a too too sullied
figure even for romance. Fail eventually where you must,
gossamer first applies those certain accidents of birth
hilariously gratuitous with wings like harvest moons,
infinitely hesitant to advance one's last contrivance.
Juggle increasingly what the weather must before wanting
knowledge just of the crime, the motive basically a
lingering keepsake of an ill-timed competition,
mere longing for which doesn't inspire confidence or
nothing more sublime. Chop chop on company time the empire
of nonchalance is now confined to clouds in your pants,
purple onion and an echoing dance where a turning stair was
quite possibly accommodated. Who can believe that the
right question won't tow barges past the river god, big and
solemn, rolling breathtakingly to a salty end?
This sure beats wondering about the top of the stairs
undoing that meager sense of childhood in a leering face,
very unusual for the afternoon, that heartache
without variation, three or four consultations for
extracting which disappointment likely to rub the most.
Yes, exactly a second-stringer lost in a dream, who is you
zanier, yes, excluding chance, than anyone may fathom.

Xystus

Almost in that happiest place teasing rain from wrong
but gladly will not as we are much too jubilant to
care there being some fifty variations of warblers O.
Don't stop, please, the shadows are no longer at the door.
Even so misterioso, near jumping at the moon's
fading correspondence, the very delirium
gentlemen and clichés forever humble, my dear
half-lit Susannah, our elders expose their wrinkled joy
in nonchalance, their emptiness expert in that tempo.
Jiggle your heart awhile like leopard sin ablaze with
knowing hunger downright random to our wilderness.
Let anyone enter, your smile a window to my abstinence
more from alibis or silence than dissolution,
north by far of those omnivorous Nevadas everyday
occupied by the dizzy chan chan of desert winds.
Promise no empty paradise of judgment without some
quite tender crime of complicity on our frontier of
repetition, a mauve dawn not quite the likeness of
skin willing the comforting and luscious distances
to approaching this memory of absolving time.
Unusually restless in my desire to step the house
voicing the shades, the common evil that dares prophecy,
who comes and goes only a matter of lemons in the fog.
X looks delirious with longing for your dreamy boulevards.
You can't deny it, the afternoon's perfectly angled to
zigzag our play, our careless dancing almost faithfully.

Yes

An impulse, a crowded dream brightening without flame,
besides anyone chancing everyday delirium
chasing the giddy inside hungriest for kisses.
Dallying in a certain light, anonymous doorways,
empty glow downtown circles the high, briefest ceiling.
Facing the echo twice he cases the beautiful ambush
galaxies away, howling memory, leaning on
heart-sore Lazaruses more than obliging opinion or
itchy purgatories quickly resembling a stranger
juggling lemons minus nostalgia for starry nights.
Keeping close to the wall he slips between the curtains
listening for a step or the feel of air near the open passage,
mockingbird somewhere nattering an olden prophecy.
No, he knew the chase of that darling flesh, everything
of the whisper, the wounded smile, the crowd of sinners
passing justice, peeking from lowered eyes as they enter
quietly the flowing house. Laconic mountaintops or pert
rows of tantalizing tomatoes or mashed potatoes
something something the simple life, as he kisses the hands of
those two graces on the couch with a brown, silly dog,
urgently given the sanctity of returning home,
vainglorious tabernacle that he might spill now
with that unsatisfied wound, that wilderness in his heart.
Exactly X willing the ding-ding-ding-ding-ding-a-ling-a,
yes, with your work and someone who loves you genuinely much,
zip zap, pretty blue skyligt outpacing the element.

Zucchetto

A slow light that is more than clarity
a little like admitting your tender opposite
bleary-eyed and victorious at least
where strings of lilies and lions meet.
Admitting broken contrivances,
elements long ago faded from the dusty,
bitter night, the negation of all that promises
to win us home. Hi-ya-yaya,
how almost willingly ordinary as friends
or what someone else is typically doing
this very morning rum-tum-tum without skin,
things in play west on Beverly east on Beverly
before dreaming any future place.
Ablaze with alabaster one must admit
as long as there is near music kicking around
nowhere more winsome than in the outlandish passage
from April to California, Sunday to Jose, March to French
and all the wilderness and Septembers in between.
Slow ghost thicket, a tempo of someone's own,
please please the quintessentially readymade
and risen stranger, the tremor in the house,
rather than some unfinished crime without dragon
or alibi in the drowsy garden.
O savage, O brightening Niagara,
O briefest, fussy thing in ruffled light,
wait, I'm a stranger here myself.

JOHN HUMBLE | *Shooting L.A.*

> *It was a splendid day in Spring*
> *and outside we could hear the birds*
> *that hadn't been killed*
> *by the smog*[1]

If you've never been to Los Angeles, but you have some kind of image of it in your head, it's probably wrong. There are any number of clichéd notions of what L.A. is, but no concept of this city could prepare you for the reality.

Let's start with some facts about L.A. One very interesting fact about Los Angeles is that it's the first minority-majority city in the U.S. and hosts the largest populations of Iranians, Armenians, Filipinos, Guatemalans, Hungarians, Israelis, Koreans, Mexicans, Salvadorans, and Thais in the world outside of their respective countries. Many of these people have imported much of their culture and lifestyles to L.A., and in particular, their authentic cuisine. Simply said, I've eaten my way though L.A. while I've been working in these communities with my camera.

A prime example of this is the Wat Thai in North Hollywood. This is a Buddhist temple that looks like it was sent, piece-by-piece, from Bangkok. It is complete with orange-robed monks, fearsome totems at the doors and, on weekends, lots of small stands selling delicious, inexpensive Thai home cooking. Being at the temple on the weekend is as close as you can get to Thailand without stepping on a plane.

This polyglot character of Los Angeles is because people from more than 140 countries, who speak at least 224 languages, inhabit the city. Many areas of the city are actually named for the high concentration of ethnic people who live there; Koreatown and Little Tokyo come to mind. Los Angeles is also one of the most religiously diverse locations in the world.

The Port of Los Angeles and Long Beach is the most important in the U.S., and one of the most significant ports in the world. L.A. is the largest manufacturing center in the U.S. and, were it a country, Los Angeles would have the 10th largest economy in the world. It is also the most car-populated metropolis in the world with about one car per 1.8 people. And, the commuters in these cars journey a collective migration of about 100 million miles a day, much of it on one of the largest freeway systems in the world.

Los Angeles, in spite of much improvement, still has some of the dirtiest air in the nation and, lest we forget, fires, mudslides, and the occasional earthquake and riot.

But, despite all of this, what still attracts mass migrations of people here, is the lifestyle of Southern California; the sun (325 days a year), the ocean and mountains (you can surf in the morning and ski in the afternoon), and the still real possibility of realizing the American Dream.

Hollywood still beckons, with its promise to make you young and rich overnight. The clubs teem with bands from all over the world hoping there is an A & M agent in the audience who'll send them on their way to fame. The headshot factories don't lack for fresh faces in need of a nicely retouched portrait to shop around. The entertainment industry still attracts dreamers and opportunists alike.

All of this is what I stepped into with my camera in the mid-1970s. I came to do this through a most circuitous route. My father was in the U.S. Army, so I saw much of America, and a few foreign countries, from the window of a moving car. Not to mention, of course, that I lived in quite a few of those places.

I never had any experience with cameras until, when I was 23, I was drafted into the U.S. Army. I bought a little 35mm camera and began photographing my surroundings. I was absolutely amazed at the fidelity and veracity of the images so, after being discharged, I went to college and got a job photographing for the student newspaper. This led, after graduation, to a job as a photographer at the *Washington Post*.

At that time, I had a great determination to pursue my own work, so I left the *Post* and studied at the San Francisco Art Institute. That was truly an eye-opening experience for someone as grounded in the realities of photojournalism as I was. Suddenly there were no clear guidelines, no certainties, and I was free to depict the world in any way that I liked. That opportunity to explore the medium and my relation to it was crucial to the way I see now.

After leaving San Francisco, I decided that I wanted to see and learn about as much of the world as possible, so I went to Amsterdam and bought a vw van. I lived in that van for a year and a half while I traveled though Europe, the Middle East, Africa and Asia. At the end of the trip I traded the van for 6 Turkish carpets in the bazaar in Istanbul, and came home.

So, I came to Los Angeles and started teaching, but I never really got used to this place. It never seemed to take on the familiarity that causes most people to stop looking. Someone who makes the same drive everyday, for example, soon stops actually looking at the scenery as they go through it. A picture on the wall, a vase on a shelf in your home, eventually stops attracting your attention. It all just becomes part of your everyday reality. That just never seems to have happened with me and the way I look at Los Angeles.

The first photographs I made in L.A. were black and white photographs on the streets in 1975. These images were made quickly, almost intuitively, of the various street scenes I encountered. They involved trying to make a very precise image of the juxtapositions of people, cars, buildings and all the other aspects of the street in a fraction of a second. If you're familiar with Friedlander and Winogrand you know what I was after.

In addition to photographing on the streets, I also carried my Leica with me 24/7, photographing my friends, parties, places I went, in essence, pretty much anything that attracted my attention. I didn't foresee this at the time, but this provides me today with a wonderful (and poignant) diary of those years.

I made black and white pictures until 1979 when I purchased a 4 × 5 view camera, started to work in color, and turned my attention to the landscape of Los Angeles. This was financed, at first, by a grant from the National Endowment for the Arts. This fellowship was from their Documentary Survey program, and I felt that I wanted to say something more expansive about the topography of L.A. than I had been. I also knew that this body of work would wind up residing in the archives of the Museum of American Art, so I felt that I should try to create images that would deserve to be there.

You probably know that Los Angeles is a car culture. It has been said that living in Los Angeles without a car is like being a eunuch in a harem. You just can't participate. So, most of the photographs I've made of Los Angeles were first seen from a moving car. My methodology was simple; load the equipment into the car, drive around L.A. looking out the window, then stop and photograph scenes that interested me.

I really didn't start my project about L.A. with any kind of real strategy. All I knew was that I loved the ironies and paradoxes and juxtapositions of the city, and I wanted to get that on film.

So, I began driving the streets of L.A. From the manicured, manufactured facades of Beverly Hills to the seedy, graffiti-laden walls of the ramshackle communities of immigrants and the poor, I put thousands of miles on my vw van. In fact, I went through a couple of them doing that. There was a platform on top of the van, and this provided me with an ideal vantage point for many of my images, moving me up from the street-level view that most of us see all the time.

Beverly Hills, Brentwood, Bel Air; I never found that I had any interest in photographing there. There was almost no sign of life, no real character, nothing hand-made or written. Vast mansions hide behind tall walls with guard dogs and security cameras; Rodeo Drive, lined with extremely expensive stores, has no personality at all. For the most part, the people seem to be consumer robots (albeit, at the top of the consumer chain), coiffed, made-up, face-lifted, designer handbagged, Mercedes encased.

The complete opposite of all of this is true in communities such as Union-Pico, the home of many new immigrants, and East L.A., where extended second and third generations of (mostly) Latino families fill the parks on weekends for parties and many of the stores sport hand-made signs and beautiful murals on their sides, frequently featuring the Virgin of Guadalupe surrounded by items for sale in the store. The sense of life, the vibrancy of the community is palpable in these places. And, I found them irresistible, continually returning to these communities to photograph.

In the middle of this project about the landscape, I acquired two hand-held 4 × 5 cameras and began making figurative images on the streets of Los Angeles. I felt the need at that time to expand the concept of what I was depicting about Los Angeles and to create a more intimate portrait of the people who populate it. This series comprises impromptu portraits of a variety of Angelenos, including a skateboarding father and son, Eastside gang members, a Hispanic family at the beach, and a couple in wedding finery on a downtown sidewalk.

In 1999 I created a series of images that radically departed from my L.A. landscape pictures, entitled, "Lifeguard Station 26." Over a period of four months I made photographs of the ocean and sky from the same location, Lifeguard Station 26 in Santa Monica. The frame of each image is the same in that the horizon line is in the same place and the camera is pointed directly out at the ocean. All that changes is the time and the season. But the changes within the frame are dramatic, almost theatrical. While the ocean and sky are important aspects of the Los Angeles landscape, this was an opportunity to take a break from the realism of the streets of L.A., to make a series of images that were almost purely aesthetic and contemplative.

In 2001 the photo editor at the Los Angeles Times magazine called my art dealer, Jan Kesner, and asked her who she might recommend to make photographs of the L.A. River. She, of course, suggested me. While making the images of the River, I realized that, while the river occasionally showed up in my images, it usually did so in a peripheral way, as an adjunct to the landscape. I had treated the river the same way almost everyone else in L.A. does – I had ignored it.

The Los Angeles River is a purely modern construct, a perfect metaphor for the city itself. Completely artificial and the first truly twentieth-century city, Los Angeles was also the first city to create a completely artificial river. The river represents the obvious and logical result of Manifest Destiny: it was exploited to extinction, used as a dump, then entombed on an Olympian scale. But the river has a rich history and is the basic reason for the location of the city itself. It has influenced the city's history and culture more than any other single entity. I realized that this was my next project.

Three hundred years ago the L.A. River was a wild river, flowing through a lush, fertile landscape of forests and marshlands teeming with wildlife and waterfowl, providing sustenance for the first settlements of Indians. It was not always benign: during winter rains it had the propensity to flood, inundating large areas of the L.A. Basin with rocks, mud and floodwater. After European settlers began to develop the area the overflow began to wreak increasingly more havoc. A particularly devastating flood in 1938 finally forced the decision to encase the length of the river – all 51 miles of it – in concrete.

Almost completely drained of water, the river had outlived its usefulness and existed only as a threat to continued expansion in the region. The purely utilitarian decision to contain it reduced it to a big, ugly, concrete ditch, with no apparent thought given to aesthetics, only the practicalities of transporting storm runoff to the sea. This it does very well, but the river is no longer a river in the true sense of the word. Little of the water flowing through its concrete channel comes from the traditional source. Instead, it is a conduit for treated wastewater and, during winter storms, a flood control channel for runoff from storm drains and the surrounding mountains.

Photographing the river was one of my arduous physical tests. Access to the river is, in some places, very restricted and difficult to get to. Then comes the task of getting my equipment and myself over walls, under wire, and down into the river. At many points the walls of the river are quite steep, making it very difficult to get into, particularly carrying a large tripod, a box containing the 4 × 5 camera and lenses, and a large bag of film holders.

343 Hillcrest Street, El Segundo, May 13, 1995

John Humble: *Shooting L.A.*　　113

1124 Anaheim Street, Wilmington, August 26, 1998

SEEING LOS ANGELES: A DIFFERENT LOOK AT A DIFFERENT CITY

2029 1ˢᵗ Street, Boyle Heights, February 26, 1998

John Humble: *Shooting L.A.*   115

3015 Wabash, East Los Angeles, October 26, 1989

5021 Felton Avenue, Hawthorne, August 17, 1991

John Humble: *Shooting L.A.*   117

12511 Venice Boulevard, Mar Vista, January 8, 1997

Hewitt Street at Palmetto Street, September 19, 2005

John Humble: *Shooting L.A.*   119

I-710 at I-105, Overpass, 2005

I-710 from I-105, Paramount, February, 1998

Selma Avenue at Vine Street, Hollywood, January 23, 1991

The Los Angeles River at The 6ᵗʰ Street Bridge, Los Angeles, 2001

View North from Pacific Coast Highway, Malibu, November 2, 1993

1920 Lincoln Boulevard, Venice, November 2, 1984

John Humble: *Shooting L.A.*   125

5041 Pico Boulevard, Los Angeles, March 12, 1985

10425 Venice Boulevard, Los Angeles, May 18, 1997

View North from the I-110, November 8, 1991

Walking in the river is only done with great caution. It tends to be slippery from the buildup of green algae and scum, and it's rife with discarded trash.

The river is a meeting place for gang-bangers, the homeless, and drug addicts. So, given its isolation, even in the midst of millions, it can be a dangerous place to be.

Given the awful ugliness of the most of the river, I decided to make images of it that were almost pictorial, beautiful photographs of an unsightly and blighted river. This seemed to be the greatest challenge that I could create in attempting to depict the river. And that is exactly what I did.

During 2006 I have been attempting to create a body of work entitled, "Sunday Afternoon." This title undoubtedly conjures idyllic scenes of people lying in hammocks, barbecueing, and having a bucolic afternoon. The pictures, however, are made in the industrial sections of Los Angeles on Sunday afternoons when they are, for the most part, deserted. These industrial areas, so full of life six days a week, are rendered almost as stage sets by the lack of people and activity.

I say that I am "trying" to create this body of work, because police and security guards are making this very difficult to do. And, the police don't actually have to drive by and see me photographing, some concerned citizen will call them on a cell-phone and report my "suspicious activity."

Before 9/11 I had very little contact with the police when I was working. Now, I have some kind of contact with the police almost every time I go out. I was pulled over, for example, a couple of months ago, in the Port of Long Beach; Port Police, Harbor Patrol and a security van, lights flashing, etc. They asked for ID, ran it, and questioned me about what I was doing. Usually the police check me out and, when they realize that I have no terrorist designs, we go our separate ways. Since I use a large camera, on a tripod, I'm quite obvious and attract attention when I'm working.

My most recent contact with the police was on August 20, 2006.

I was making a photograph in the center median of Alameda Street (which is quite wide at that point), in Carson, by the train tracks, and I wasn't there two minutes before a Sheriff's car pulled up on one side of me and another on the other side. They ordered me to come to them showing my hands, made me stand against the cruiser with my feet spread and my hands behind my back (that they held), while they asked me if I had anything on me, patted me down and emptied my pockets. They asked me for ID and I told them it was in the truck and they got it. In the meantime they made me sit in the back of the cruiser with my hands on the cage and the door closed. I tried to explain that I was only making a photograph, but they ignored me.

The officers told me that it was unlawful to photograph in that area, but I politely told them that I have been doing this for 30 years, and I'm pretty sure I was not in violation of any law. Realizing that I knew my rights, they didn't press that issue, but went into the usual 9/11 terrorism routine. So, they finally let me out of the car, gave me my things back, and said I had to get off the median. They also thanked me for being cooperative – as though I had a choice.

While I always explain my rights to the officers who question me, it has become unnerving and I feel a high degree of tension every time I go into the streets to photograph. I understand the security concerns of the police, but I tell them that it is very unlikely that a potential terrorist would stand on a public sidewalk with a 4 × 5 camera on a tripod, in broad daylight, in order to pursue terrorist activity. I would make an image with my cell-phone camera and attract no attention at all. I also inform that I could get a much better and more detailed image of the area I'm photographing by using Google Earth in the privacy of my own home.

Over the years, I've occasionally been threatened with physical violence (including death), been confronted by gangs, rousted by police and security guards, and yelled at by angry homeowners and business owners.

But all in all, I can't think of a better subject to have embraced with my camera than Los Angeles. I've gained a great admiration and respect for this unplanned and grand experiment in progress. I've seen the most remarkable things and met the most remarkable people, and I've learned a lot about a myriad of cultures and lifestyles. And I think I've made some photographs that depict what I feel is the real Los Angeles.

Rollin' down the Imperial Highway
With a big nasty redhead at my side
Santa Ana winds blowin' hot from the north
And we was born to ride

Roll down the window put down the top
Crank up the Beach Boys baby
Don't let the music stop
We're gonna ride it till we just can't ride it no more

From the South Bay to the Valley
From the West Side to the East Side
Everybody's very happy
'Cause the sun is shining all the time
Looks like another perfect day

I Love L.A.[2]

NOTES

1   Charles Bukowski, from "Burning in Water, Drowning in Flame."
2   Randy Newman, "I Love L.A."

© RMcN

MICHEL BULTEAU | *Two Poems*

Marilyn Monroe's Daughter

Debbie never liked L.A.
Afraid of being held prisoner in a fortress
At the top of the hill
With a swimming pool
And a few modern paintings to brighten up the walls.
"Can you imagine William S. Burroughs, living here,
On the lunar surface, writing scripts
For Hollywood?" she said.
"The slate he's made of wouldn't do
for the studios' sober, classic modeling.
Just like you, as a matter of fact." I respond.
Today, Debbie is back from Los Angeles.
The band played at the Whiskey A Go-Go.
She is a bit tired, vulnerable as always.
And proud to announce that John Cassavetes
Came to film the concert.
"And do you know who the cameraman was?" she adds.
"Sam Shaw, the one who shot Marilyn
On the subway grate
When her dress is whipped up."
Her eyes flutter.
Debbie too is a radiant child.
What a feeling, to hug
The one who, just a short while ago,
Got me to believe she was Marilyn Monroe's daughter!

Stars

We can consider Los Angeles as self-evident,
That's what I did for a long time.
Then I finally got over the contempt
That most New Yorkers have for it.
Understanding comes slowly,
Often in confusion,
Most often in flashes.
We tell ourselves that the climate is favorable,
That it is the promised land for tired desperados
And that weariness has invaded all.
That is not exactly right.
In the Last Tycoon,
F. Scott Fitzgerald's last unfinished book
There is a very powerful, very secret scene:
The one where Monroe Stahr,
Having driven Kathleen home,
Gets back in his car
And listens within himself
To what could be the work of an unknown composer...
That music attracts us,
We poor emerald moths poisoned by the dream factory.
There follows the names of some fifty stars
And thirty mythical places
That have always belonged to us,
Prevented our frailty from collapsing
Like a tent in a storm.

Eccentric Donald what possessed you
To want to shoot in Hollywood?
To fall in love with a fourteen year old?
To not beat Brando at arm wrestling?
To shoot yourself in the head
In your apartment on Crescent Drive
The same gunshot that killed Turner in *Performance*?

Translated by Béatrice Mousli

GUY BENNETT | *The Los Angeles Literary Landscape:*
A Core Sample

They say that Los Angeles is a city hostile to writers. That it is a literary desert, a cultural wasteland, an intellectual black hole. The metaphors may vary but the underlying argument, simplistic though it may be, remains constant; it goes like this: the presence of Hollywood is so deleterious, the weight of the entertainment-industrial complex so overwhelming, that any not-for-profit creative endeavor will inevitably be contaminated and is thus doomed to failure by mere proximity. In light of this, "independent" (which in the U.S. has tellingly come to mean "non-corporate") cultural activity is frequently described in terms that seem more appropriate for resistance fighters waging a guerilla war against a foreign occupier, than for artists and writers actually making work. Thus one does not speak of writing in Los Angeles, but of writing "in the shadow of Hollywood," "in the belly of the beast," etc., all of which is true to a certain extent. At least on the surface.

Were we to judge Los Angeles-based literary activity on its sheer visibility, that is, on what we see and hear around us, whether on TV or radio, in newspapers or magazines, we would have to conclude that there is in fact little or nothing happening there, since only rarely does word of it ever enter the sphere of public discourse. If we dig beneath the surface, however, we need to revise that judgment. And, as with most things, the deeper we dig, the greater the revision we need to make. So, if we were to take a core sample of Los Angeles' literary landscape, what would we find?

Well, on the surface, that is, what the public can see without having to look for it, is the occasionally well-publicized reading, lecture, or interview, usually by a "best-selling" writer from somewhere else, whose latest book has just been published by a commercial press and whose presence among us was conjured for the sole purpose of promoting it, that is, of selling copies. Not surprisingly, these events tend to take place in bookstores, where the product is at hand and the cash register not far away. The idea that there might be a literary event whose primary focus is on anything other than the commerce of writing seems to be unheard of in the public sphere. Indeed, the single "official" literary fair – *The Los Angeles Times Festival of Books,* touted on its own website as "America's largest and grandest literary event" – is a veritable Disneyland of the book trade, with decorated booths, food stands, costumed characters, and activities for children. Oh yes, and readings and book signings, too. An unapologetic example of the commodification of literary culture, it is to the traditional book fair – such as the *Marché de la poésie,* which opens here in Paris today [June 15, 2006] – what Barnes & Noble and Borders, who are among its many corporate sponsors, are to the "independent" (there's that word again!) bookstore: a hypercapitalist wolf in literary sheep's clothing.

To come back to our core sample: just below the surface, one becomes aware of a number of other literary events, mostly in the form of occasional readings and discussions, taking place at a variety of public venues, from the L.A. Central Library to various local museums – the Armand Hammer Museum, The Getty Center, The Skirball Cultural Center, etc. These, too, are aimed at the general public, though they lack the hyperbole, razzle-dazzle, and family-friendliness of the above-mentioned festival. Similar events regularly take place on local college campuses (Cal Poly Pomona, Otis College of Art and Design, USC, UCLA, etc.), though these are attended primarily by students, and announcements rarely reach beyond the campus communities. There are also at least two Los Angeles-based literary programs broadcast on local radio stations: "Bookworm" on KCRW and the "Poet's Café" on KPFK, though both take place weekday afternoons when most people work and are therefore unable to listen to them. All of these events feature fiction writers as well as poets, ranging from the well-known to not so well-known; only occasionally do they feature Angeleno writers, however.

A bit deeper in terms of visibility is the Beyond Baroque Literary Arts Center, the only such institution in Los Angeles. Since 1969, it has featured regular readings, workshops, and performances of a distinctly non-commercial, non-academic nature. As such, it tends to draw people more interested in writing as it's happening now, than in getting their book signed or having their picture taken with the author. It is on this level – ironically, well below the general public's threshold of perception – that the literary landscape begins to reflect and engage the local writing community, for Beyond Baroque and the venues that follow regularly present Los Angeles-based writers, who figure prominently in their schedule of events. The center also operates a bookstore, which stocks titles by a surprising variety of small and micro presses from across the country, as well as a number of literary magazines, both local and not, and houses an archive of small press books and chapbooks, as well as audio recordings of many of the events it has hosted over the years. Beyond Baroque occasionally organizes small press festivals and conferences, which are in many ways the antithesis of the Los Angeles Times Festival of Books because the emphasis is actually on writing and publishing, as opposed to marketing and selling, the most recent of which took place three weeks ago, on May 29th, and featured presentations by the editors of eight local small presses and magazines, and readings by their authors.

This would be a good place to say a word or two about the local presses, which are legion, for what the city lacks in large, commercial publishers, it more than makes up for in small and micro presses. According to Len Fulton, publisher of the small press directory *Dustbooks*, there are some 150 small presses and several dozen literary magazines based in Los Angeles. To highlight just a few we could mention Beyond Baroque Books, the publishing arm of the literary center I have just spoken of; Cloverfield Books, which specializes in works of short fiction; Green Integer, which perhaps the largest of the local small presses, publishing fiction, non-fiction, and poetry; Make Now Press, a new press publishing Oulipian and other constraint-based work, Red Hen Press, which focuses exclusively on Los Angeles-based writers, my own Seeing Eye Books, which publishes chapbooks of contemporary international poetry, and publisher of the present volume, Seismicity Editions, with its program of poetry, fiction, and critical essays, both in the English original and in translation.

At the very bottom of the core sample are those events that get little to no public exposure, and that you are not likely to be aware of unless you are on the mailing list, frequent the club, bar, or café that hosts them, or personally know the organizers or readers. These events tend to feature local writers reading from current or recent projects, and thus constitute a kind of collective work-in-progress of writing being done around the city. Though they are too numerous to list here (there's a fairly thorough calendar at www.poetix.net), I would like to highlight a few of those doing interesting or unusual things. For starters, the "Last Sunday Readings at The Smell," a series of poetry readings that take place on the last Sunday of the month at a club ("The Smell") located in a downtown warehouse. These readings generally bring together four poets, and have also included live music and projections of experimental films. There is also "Tongue and Groove," another "last Sunday" reading series, this time dedicated to contemporary fiction, which takes place in the Hotel Café on Cahuenga in Hollywood (or should we say "in the belly of the beast"?). I would also like to mention the "L.A.-Lit" series of interviews with and readings by primarily Angeleno poets that take place at BetaLevel, a bomb-shelter-like space located beneath an alleyway in Chinatown; these are recorded live and later made available for listening or downloading on their website at www.la-lit.com.

And then there are the even more improbable and/or invisible events, such as the Los Angeles Metro "Poetry in Motion" project, which organizes readings in bus and subway stations throughout the city during the month of April (National Poetry Month); and last

October's "Fossil Fuel Fossil" event, described as "a guided poem by bicycle through Los Angeles," for which people were invited to meet at Angel's Flight, a disused funicular in downtown L.A., then bicycle through the city to an accompaniment of poems; and the "Long Beach Notebook" reading series, which takes place in the home of a local poet who lives in Naples, Long Beach, "a real live island replete with canals, gondolas and cascades of night blooming jasmine," in the words of the host and organizer of the series.

Clearly, there is a lot going on, though very little of it ever meets the public eye. With a bit of effort, however, one finds that there is a dynamic, if dispersed, "scene" in which local writing actually engages and informs the city, as unlikely as that may seem. Brecht once remarked about Los Angeles, "Scratch a bit, and the desert comes through." Like the desert, the literary landscape of Los Angeles may appear barren at first, especially to those looking at it from afar or just driving through, but those who've taken the trouble to explore the desert know that there's a lot more to it than just sand and rocks.

© RMcN

DAVID JAMES | *Los Angeles, Writing and Space*

for Nicole Brenez

Since I am talking about Los Angeles here in Paris, I will use a methodology inaugurated in Paris.[1] Though the cites are at least half-way to being antipodes, Los Angeles has a strong, what might be called "geo-intellectual," connection with Paris in that the theory of the social significance of space formulated by Henri Lefebvre bore some of its best fruit in the work of the Los Angeles School of geographers.[2] I will take advantage of that association to propose a spatial reading of the history of literature in Los Angeles and argue that the paradigms by which its urban specificity has been modeled also illuminate literary developments.

This thesis is initially justified in that so much writing in Los Angeles shows such an overriding preoccupation with a sense of its own place that the architectural texture of the city becomes itself the primary subject matter and the model of psychological self-consciousness. Spatiality – the geographical given and the human transformation and re-imagining of it – appears as the bed-rock upon which the specifics of social life are constructed, the frame within which cultural sensibility finds itself. One sign of this is the plethora of literary anthologies that nominate the city itself as their frame of reference. My own, amateur enthusiast's library, for instance, contains a dozen, widely divergent, such anthologies, all published in the thirty-five years since the groundbreaking *Anthology of L.A. Poets* in 1972, and almost all with a similarly titular emphasis on the city.[3] Rather than pursuing this spatial grounding numerically, let me give a couple of examples from poets represented at this conference:

Martha Ronk, one of the very few writers to appear in many of these anthologies, titled her first collection of poems, *Desire in L.A.*,[4] as if to affirm that the most primary and organic interiority was to be understood as positioned by the city outside; similarly, the poetry that Guy Bennett contributed to the most recent of them, consists of "Eight Architectural Miniatures,"[5] short visually-precise descriptions of houses in the city, that resemble nothing so much as Judy Fiskin's lapidary photographs of Los Angeles domestic buildings in the current *Los Angeles 1955–1985, Naissance d'une capitale artistique* exhibition at the Centre Pompidou, which is itself a similarly spatialized conception of the city as cultural vortex. Whatever the analytic value of these examples, the fact remains that in the last quarter century, geographical paradigms compatible with if not derived directly from Lefebvre's insistence on the primacy of space in the human sciences have transformed the way we think *in* Los Angeles as well how we think *about* Los Angeles.

I will be concerned with two of these spatial paradigms, one that dominated until around 1970 and one that has gradually displaced it since.

Los Angeles used to be a despised and anomalous place, a reproach to civilized urbanity. Until the last quarter of the twentieth century, their city's defining feature was thought to be the lateral dispersal across the desert plains that formed it as an agglomeration of separate and often isolated communities, and so inhibited the vertical development chief characteristic of New York and Chicago which maintained the population density and the sidewalk interaction of the American urban melting pot. This spatiality and its implications were supposed to be reciprocated culturally: Los Angeles's lack of a vertical architectural dimension corresponded to its lack of modernism's cultural hierarchies, specifically the lack of a high culture and the ubiquity of the low.

Contrary to common assumptions, L.A.'s dispersed spatiality does not reflect the lack of a civic center; the downtown area always has been and still is, not only the spatial center, but also the economic, financial and administrative core.[6] And it was also the location of the city's most prominent industry, the movies. Even when the studios moved from their earliest location at Seventh and Olive a few miles to the north-west and eventually to Hollywood, given the scale of the city as a whole, they remained close to the geographical center, whence they provided the focus for all the city's other cultural activity. Remote from the North Atlantic axis that oriented prototypical high modernist American writers such as T.S. Eliot and Ezra Pound to Europe, literature in Los Angeles in the middle third of the century continued to be a dependency and an adjunct of what, since Theodore W. Adorno coined the term in Los Angeles during his exile in the 1940s, has been known as the culture industry.[7] While San Francisco proved responsive to post-war modernisms, especially the jazz and abstract expressionism of the beat era, writing in Los Angeles was directed by "the business," by Hollywood.

I will designate this mid-century Los Angeles writing, "industrial literature," conjoining in that term both its source in the film industry and the fact that its primary form, the screenplay, more closely approached the assembly line model of industrial production than any other form of writing; in the classic period of the Hollywood studio-system, most screenplays were written and rewritten by many hands, resulting in what, as Simone de Beauvoir noted in her account of her visit to the city in the 1947, "a division of labor so extreme that no one has a hold on the complete work."[8] Screen and television writing remains the city's best known and best paid form of writing, and one that is organized on an industrial scale: every fall, for example, the city hosts a "Screenwriting Expo" attended by between four and five thousand writers.[9]

This industrial writing began in earnest in the 1930s when the introduction of sound first created the need for film dialogue, forcing the studios to bring in New York playwrights and celebrated novelists from the east. F. Scott Fitzgerald, William Faulkner, and others so transplanted resented the assembly-line production and the studio bosses' disregard for their individual voices and value systems. In reaction they inaugurated the second form of industrial writing, the Hollywood novel – *The Day of the Locust* (Nathanael West, 1933), *What*

Makes Sammy Run (Budd Schulberg, 1941), *The Last Tycoon* (F. Scott Fitzgerald, 1948), and so on – which remains the best-known form of literature associated with the city.

The third kind of industrial writing transfigured the lowest form of literature, pulp fiction, to create a noir tradition of detective and police novels in which film and literature have fertilized each other ever since. Begun in the early thirties by James M. Cain and Horace McCoy, the tradition peaked in the screenplays and novels of Raymond Chandler, with his *The Little Sister* (1949) – in which he expressed his hatred of equally of both the city and its industry – marking the convergence of the Hollywood and the hard-boiled detective novel. Its description of Marlowe's evening drive from Sunset Boulevard, over the Cahuenga Pass and out through the San Fernando Valley to Malibu, and then his return to the city ("I smelled Los Angeles before I got to it") where he goes to the cinema, is only most succinct of his many seminal negative odes in which the urban fabric and the movies each become metaphors for the other's hollow depravity.

Chandler's greatest creativity ended with the McCarthy era and the blacklist that extirpated almost all dissenting culture in Los Angeles until the mid 1960s, but his work has been the most important point of reference, both positive and negative, for contemporary neo-noir industrial fiction, which continues the his symbiotic love-hate relation with the movies and the city. The novels of James Ellroy and Walter Mosley, as well as of more straightforwardly generic writers such as Michael Connelly, Robert Crais, and T. Jefferson Parker, all mobilize cinematic narrative codes; they return to the industry in the form of movies adapted from them, and all the writers also work extensively for film and television. The career of Walter Mosley, the creator of the series of noir novels featuring an African American sleuth, Easy Rawlins is exemplary. Though with his first success he relocated to the East Coast, since the filming of his novel, *Devil in a Blue Dress* in 1995 – for which he was an associate producer – he has worked in Hollywood as a producer, writer, and actor, as well as appearing as himself in television shows.[10]

The mutual fertilization of noir literary practices in and on the margins of Hollywood is not entirely uninflected or without modernist critiques of mass culture. Somewhere the field has to find a place for Bertolt Brecht's screenplays, written while he lived in Santa Monica during World War II, for Kenneth Anger's scabrous exposé, *Hollywood Babylon* (even though he had to come to Paris to write it), or poet Charles Bukowski's comic novel, *Hollywood*, in which he described his role in the production of a film about himself and his myth.[11] Even before Clement Greenberg formulated the avant-garde-kitsch binary, it was fundamental in Hollywood noir's founding masterpiece, *The Day of the Locust*, in which the protagonist's painting, "The Burning of Los Angeles," is a representation of Hollywood's decadence but is itself painted in the idioms of the European masters. The novel itself aspires to a similar high-cultural status – even if it was eventually made into a successful film. And (thanks at least initially to French critics), film noir is itself today regarded as the most refractory of Hollywood genres.

This said, mid-century Los Angeles writing was largely low and flat, circumscribed by and oriented to Hollywood. Very little other writing of major significance appeared other than in the industry's penumbra. Since the late 1960s, Hollywood's centrality in and influence over the cultural life of the city as whole has continued to grow, but new forms of writing have emerged into an unexpected prominence. Fundamentally amateur and working-class where the other was professional, and to an unprecedented degree, anti- or para-industrial rather than industrial, these writings are not subtended by the high/low binary. Rather, reflecting the energies of more or less self-sufficient enclaves of substantial spatial and cultural autonomy that provide sustenance apart from the culture industries, they both transcend and deconstruct modernist cultural hierarchies. To frame these, I turn again return to geography.

Since the 1960s, Los Angeles iconic stature has been transformed, with the combined impact of two developments making it a prototypical rather than an anomalous city: the re-theorized by geographers of the significance of its structure and the revitalization by immigration of its multi-ethnic complexity. In retrospect, the turning point in the former appears to be the intervention of the English art and architecture critic, Reyner Banham. His *Los Angeles: The Architecture of Four Ecologies*, first published in 1971 (the year before *Anthology of L.A. Poets*), broke new ground because it celebrated the city's specificity in its own terms, rather than denigrating it as a dystopian parody of previous forms of urbanity; Banham's recognition that "it is difficult to register the total artefact as a distinctive human construct because there is nothing else with which to compare it, and thus no class into which it may be pigeonholed"[12] allowed him to perceive Los Angeles as the product of its topographic given and its historical development from the Mexican Ranchos through to the Pop art present – precisely the interaction of geography and culture that informed Lefebvre's model of spatiality. With the ground thus prepared, Soja and the Los Angeles geographers were able to rehabilitate a tradition of commentary on the distinctiveness of the city's separate communities that began in the late nineteenth century (when already it was recognized that Los Angeles was "made up of groups who often live in isolated communities" all with "their own customs, language, and religious habits and associations"[13]), and especially to Carey McWilliams's mid-century description of it as an "Archipelago" of "social and ethnic islands, economically interrelated but culturally disparate." McWilliams, the city's most prescient analyst, summarily proposed that Los Angeles contained a "racial and cultural rectangle: White, Negro, Mexican, and Oriental."[14]

Since then and especially since the early 1970s, this demographic rectangle has been transformed as the numbers of what were the three minority groups have grown enormously. In 1970, there were almost five million whites in Los Angeles or 70% of the city; one million Latinos made up 15%; ³/₄ million blacks made 11%; and ¹/₄ million Asians, 4%. Thirty years later at the turn of the millennium the proportion of whites to minorities had been inverted: Anglos were down to 31.0% – the percentage of all minorities combined in 1970 –

and blacks were down slightly to 10%, while nearly 5 million Latinos comprised 45.0% of the total and 1.7 million Asians, 15%, the last two having increased by factors of almost three and five respectively.[15] Los Angeles now has larger and more self-contained communities of African-, Mexican-, and Asian Americans than any other city, and whites are a minority. More so than in any previous conurbation, the city's lateral dispersal has allowed these communities, not only to maintain their own cultural traditions, but also to renew them and now to force them upon the attention of the city at large.

Reinforced by and reinforcing the hegemony of identity politics in academic humanities and sociology programs, this demographic transformation has made ethnicity the major cultural frame of reference and given ethnically identified writers an unprecedented prestige and cultural leverage. But it has not regenerated the modernist model in which an industrial base was confronted by a bourgeois mandarin high culture. Instead it engendered self-consciously minority communities, islands outside and to a degree independent and even suspicious of industrial writing. And though most of these islands are ethnically-specific, some parallel commonalities are formed by gender or sexuality while others are purely cultural.[16] Such identity-based writing was not, of course, without precedent, either in self-consciously local writing nor even within the noir tradition. The beat scene that flourished around the Venice West café and *From the Ashes: Voices of Watts*,[17] Budd Schulberg's collection of African American writing from the workshop he organized in Watts after the 1965 rebellion, are particularly important precursors of the former; while Chester Himes' novel about a young black man fighting racial prejudice in the wartime shipyards, *If He Hollers, Let Him Go* (1946), and John Rechy's autobiographical novel about a hustler, *City of Night* (1963), could be seen as antecedents to African American and Chicano literature respectively, with *City of Night* also important as pioneering gay novel – though neither has ever been made into a movie!

The emergence of writing by people of color could be demonstrated in several ways: for example, by listing important names in each of the three main ethnic groups and by listing the titles they published, but my guess is that most are unknown here, with the exception of Wanda Coleman, an African-American woman whose work most clearly displays a working-class ethnic rather than avant-gardist alterity to the industry and who has read recently in Paris. But something of the significance of their emergence can be gleaned from differences in the anthologies that followed the inaugural, *Anthology of L.A. Poets*. Of the sixty-two poets collected in the next major anthology, Bill Mohr's 1985, *Poetry Loves Poetry*, six or 10% were people of color and one third were women. And four years later a watershed was reached with the small-press publication of several volumes by minority poets and the breakthrough anthology, *Invocation L.A. Urban Multicultural Poetry*. Edited by a Black woman, Michelle T. Clinton, a Hispanic woman, Naomi Quiñonez, and a mixed Japanese and Hispanic American man, Sesshu Foster, its preface claimed it to be the first that "truly represents the multicultural character of the city," with more than half the poets being women.[18] Since then, anthologies of Los Angeles writing have reflected the polemics of multiculturalism itself, some giving ample samplings of ethnic writers, while others, especially those with a commitment to high modernist poetics, considerably less.[19]

The tension among incommensurate aesthetics and the cultural dispersal instanced in recent anthologies of L.A. poetry and writing generally is also ironically illustrated by one feature they all share, that is, the editor always prominently includes his (and apart from the two women of color who collaborated in editing *Invocation L.A.*, they are all men) own writing as a prime example of the principles that subtend the collection and indeed sometimes take a self-congratulatory pride in their differences from the others. More than half of the first page of one of them, for example, an anthology of putatively "innovative poetry in Southern California" but actually almost entirely of work broadly within post-L:A:N:G:U:A:G:E formalism, is comprised of a lengthy, self-congratulatory footnote in which the editor pointedly discusses the contents of half dozen other anthologies, but only to demonstrate how infrequently their selections overlap with his own.[20] The anthologies, then, are typically strategic interventions that mobilize and publicize the work of the editor and his cultural group – distinct cultural factions or islands that reflect spatial fragmentation.[21]

This dispersal of the social and spatial field of writing by which the margins become multiple alternative centers suggests many avenues for further analysis; but to conclude here let me sketch half a dozen possibilities:

1. The investigation of the relationship between the various minority communities and Hollywood itself. Though usually hidden rather than foregrounded in minority writing, the industrial center is still so powerful that ethnic and cultural enclaves are almost never entirely free of either its influence or its compelling attraction; indeed to suppose they might be would be to overlook the prominence of culture in contemporary society and the culture industries' role in reproducing capitalism's enabling social and ideological preconditions. Paul Vangelisti specifies the consequent dialectic of repulsion and desire when he notes that writers in L.A. are either involved in Hollywood or trying to keep their distance from it – and its never clear which of these is the more difficult.[22] Tracking more or less ambivalent reference to industrial culture in minority practices is a relatively simple matter of content analysis; but the more difficult question is the evaluation of their use of collage, reflexive, and other modernist structures that were once thought to be radically subversive but which have now become the logic of the culture industries themselves. It no longer possible to be clear whether the appearance of such strategies in disaffiliated poetics indicate dissent of some kind or merely the mark of Hollywood's colonization of textual practices ostensibly outside its purview. Frank Chin's novel, *Gunga Din Highway* supplies a road-map through this territory, brilliantly demonstrating how the plurivocality of Chinese American writing is anticipated in the movies and constantly shadowed by them, and that much of what passes for autonomous ethnic identity was in fact constructed from prior media images.[23]

2. The investigation of the differences among the characteristics
and determinants of the various cultural enclaves. How do, say,
African American and Asian American writing reflect a common
minoritarian situation or problematic, and how do their respective
histories, cultural traditions, spatialities, and so on result in, not simply
a variety of formal resources, but fundamentally a-parallel aesthetics.
Once begun, such a comparative study will have to be endlessly
subdivided, for the ethnic categories themselves have proliferated
and are all further divisible in gender and sexual terms. Thus, for
example, Asian American used to be a relatively non-problematical
identity, one that was simply constructed on the supposed similarity
and indeed interchangeability of Chinese-, Japanese-, and Pilipino
American experience.[24] But now it has fragmented into its various
specific national origins so that the concept, "Asian American" has
lost whatever coherence as an object of theoretical knowledge it
might once have had, and must now more properly be regarded as
a "fiction."[25] Similarly, ethnic specificity has been further subdivided
in sexual terms as male, female, gay, lesbian, bi, and so on. Hence
what once might have been simply, Asian American writing in Los
Angeles must now be further specified as, for example heterosexual
Japanese American women's writing (such as Amy Uyematsu), and
Chinese American gay male writing (such as Russell Leong).[26]

3. The investigation of the way this range of cultural differences
produces new instabilities, but also new possibilities, in the concept
of writing itself. For example, the heritage of African oral traditions
combined with the impossibility of material possessions under
slavery clearly resulted in pronounced oral and musical emphasis
in African American culture. This remains as the heritage of para-
literary forms – folk tales, boasting, and so on – that then reappear
in hip-hop culture as a form of poetry set to music. In Los Angeles
specifically this line would extend from the Central Avenue be-bop
spoken improvisations of Slim Galliard and more recently Kamau
Daáood though to the verbal pyrotechnics of South Central Gangsta
rap. But such oral poetics are not confined to African Americans,

and other spoken word or performance poetries have thriven since the early 1980s, especially on the edges of music communities; the spoken word recording anthologies made and published by Harvey Kubernik are a remarkable testament to the vibrant mosaic of the city's popular voices – and to his own uniquely generous contribution to its culture.[27] Similarly, Mexican graphic traditions produce murals and also graffiti – which are themselves designated as "writing" – that nourish more conventionally literary forms.[28]

4. The investigation of how these minoritarian analytic projects may be turned back and brought to bear on white writing. Now that whites are a minority, outnumbered more than 4:3 by Latinos, it is both possible and necessary to displace white poetry – that is, non-industrial white writing – from the normative status it continues to claim for itself, and see it too as a determinate subcultural production. Indeed, it also breaks down into several sub-subcultures in a way parallel to the fragmented ethnic identities: a group more or less influenced by L:A:N:G:U:A:G:E poetry; punk poetry[29]; a school working in the confessional vernacular that made Charles Bukowski internationally the best-known Los Angeles poet (and a model, fortunate or not, for working-class poets everywhere), and another performance-oriented mode, the "poetry slam."[30]

5. The investigation of the international affiliations of contemporary ethnic writing. Since the Asian and Latino communities are continually being renewed and augmented by immigration, they maintain more or less active international connections, not with European traditions, either high modernist or postmodernist, but with Latin American and the Pacific Rim cultures: the "Third World." This orientation has immense implications for their various poetics. Though the ethnic communities contain pockets of great wealth (so that the gap between rich and poor in L.A. is now comparable to that in Karachi and Bombay),[31] by far the greatest numbers of the new immigrants are working-class, and so linked directly to the Third World proletariat or, to bring the terminology up to date, to the populations most exploited by post-Communist globalization. Indeed, most un- and semi-skilled

immigration into Los Angeles and indeed the U.S. generally is a direct result of neo-liberal imperialism in the south. Illegal Mexican immigration is only the most momentous of the population shifts that result from U.S. economic priorities, in this case, NAFTA's destruction of Mexican agriculture by the elimination of import barriers against the subsidized production of U.S. agribusiness. Given the scale of these and the other population movements that circulate through Los Angeles, it may be expected that eventually writing emerging from immigrant communities will be especially revelatory of world-historical social transformations.

6. The investigation of the relation between the various forms of writing and the class structure of the city. The question of class relations has been so entirely banished from cultural analysis in the U.S. that we no longer have a vocabulary for asking, let alone answering it. In Los Angeles especially, the heritage of the open-shop combined with selective de-industrialization over the last two decades, the degree of ethnic pluralism, and the strength of ethnic identity politics has continued to repress trans-ethnic working-class solidarity; in the same period, illegal immigration has created a reserve-army of unemployed that has undermined working-class organization, and a climate in which inter-ethnic hate crimes flourish.[32] The result is an extreme cultural polarization. The loss of middle-income jobs and a proportionately even greater disappearance of middle-class and mixed neighborhoods has made Los Angeles at present the most economically segregated city in the U.S.[33] Though this economic and social "Brazilianization" is a global phenomenon, the fact that it is more extreme in Los Angeles than anywhere else gives cultural workers in the city a special responsibility and a special opportunity, but one whose articulation with contemporary poetics is unclear.

Lest we think this is, if not an impossible task, then one outside the purview of innovative writing, it is worth remembering that thirty years ago the first issue of *Invisible City*, the best poetry magazine ever to have appeared in Los Angeles and the harbinger of the renaissance of poetry in the city, opened with a prose poem titled, "Why I am a

Socialist," in which the speaker (who was also the journal's editor) proposed the importance of "historical questioning" framed by "the material dialectic." [34] The cultural conditions that allowed this claim are now very remote. But if we think of what I have called "industrial writing" as writing produced by and in service of the capitalist means of cultural production, then in respect to it non-commodity minority writing may have a double potential: on the one hand, as outlaw writing that brings itself into being outside and opposed to the social boundaries that the various forms of noir attempt to police, it has a clear critical mission; on the other hand, if the different minoritarian projects – the white avant-garde as much as the gay Chinese American – can transcend their sectarian narcissism, then they may together subtend a renewal that will make the city as important in the future as a center for emancipatory popular culture as in the past it has been for industrial culture.

NOTES

1 This essay attempts to transpose to literary history the methodologies developed for cinema history in my *The Most Typical Avant-Garde: History and Geography of Minor Cinemas in Los Angeles* (Berkeley: University of California Press, 2005). It is an extended version of a talk I gave in Paris at the invitation of Béatrice Mousli and Guy Bennett. I thank them for that occasion, and also Bill Mohr for his advice and encouragement. The amount and diversity of writing produced in Los Angeles is now so enormous that a sketch as brief as this must inevitably be extremely partial.

2 The key text in the transmission of Lefebvre's ideas, particularly his notion of spatiality as socially produced and humanly imagined, was Edward W. Soja, *Postmodern Geographies: The Reassertion of Space in Critical Social Theory* (London: Verso, 1989). The "Los Angeles School" of critical, humanistic geographers coalesced at the University of California at Los Angeles around Soja; see also his *Thirdspace: Journeys to Los Angeles and Other Real-and-Imagined Places* (Cambridge, Mass.: Blackwell, 1996); and Allen J. Scott and Edward W. Soja, eds., *The City: Los Angeles and Urban Theory at the End of the Twentieth Century* (Berkeley: University of California Press, 1996). Mike Davis, himself somewhat uncomfortably attached

to the school, gives a brief overview of it in *City of Quartz: Excavating the Future in Los Angeles* (London: Verso, 1990) 84–88.

3   Bukowski, Charles, Neeli Cherry, and Paul Vangelisti, eds., *Anthology of L.A. Poets* (Los Angeles: Red Hill Press, 1972); Vangelisti's editorial innovations continued the next year with his collection of several of the same poets in *Specimen 73: A Catalogue of Poets for the Season 1973–74* (Pasadena, Ca.: Pasadena Museum of Modern Art, 1973). The others are (in chronological order): Mohr, Bill, ed., *The Streets Inside: Ten Los Angeles Poets* (Santa Monica, Ca., Momentum Press, 1978); Mohr, Bill, ed., *Poetry Loves Poetry: An Anthology of Los Angeles Poets* (Los Angeles: Momentum Press, 1985); Clinton, Michelle T., Sesshu Foster, and Naomi Quiñonez, eds., *Invocation L.A. Urban Multicultural Poetry* (Albuquerque NM.: West End Press, 1989); Fried, Elliot, ed., *Gridlock: An Anthology of Poetry About Southern California* (Long Beach: Applezaba Press, 1990); Webb, Charles Harper, *Stand Up Poetry: The Poetry of Los Angeles and Beyond* (Los Angeles: Red Wind Books, 1990); Gilbar, Steven, *L.A. Shorts* (Berkeley: Heyday Books, 1999); Vangelisti, Paul, ed., *L.A. Exiles: A Guide to Los Angeles Writing, 1932–1998* (New York: Marsilio, 1999); Ulin, David L., ed, *Another City: Writing From Los Angeles* (San Francisco, 2001); Ulin, David L., ed., *Writing Los Angeles: A Literary Anthology* (New York: Library of America, 2002); Dunn, Samantha, ed., *Women on the Edge: Writing from Los Angeles* (New Milford, CT.: Toby Press, 2005); and Messerli, Douglas, ed., *Intersections: Innovative Poetry in Southern California* (København and Los Angeles: Green Integer, 2005). Estelle Gershgoren Novak's collection, *Poets of the Non-Existent City: Los Angeles in the McCarthy Era* (Albuquerque NM.: University of New Mexico Press, 2002) is an important excavation of an otherwise lost era in the city's literary history. Sometimes the geographical focus on Los Angeles and Southern California is expanded, as for example in Ronk, Martha and Paul Vangelisti, eds., *Place as Purpose: Poetry from the Western States* (Los Angeles: Autry Museum of Western Heritage and Sun & Moon Press, 2002), and sometimes it is contracted, as for example, in *Incidental Buildings & Accidental Beauty: An Anthology of Orange County/Long Beach Poets* (Huntington Beach, Ca.: Tebot Bach 2001).

4   Ronk, Martha Clare, *Desire in L.A.* (Athens, Ga.: University of Georgia Press, 1990).

5   Messerli, ed., *Intersections* 111–114.

6   As Kevin Starr has insisted, it is "simply a myth to state that twentieth-century Los Angeles had no downtown." *Material Dreams: Southern California Through the 1920s* (New York: Oxford University Press, 1990) 78.

7   See Max Horkheimer and Theodor W. Adorno, *Dialectic of Enlightenment*, trans. John Cumming (New York; Herder and Herder, 1972).

8 *America Day by Day* (Berkeley: University of California Press, 1999) 118.

9 http://www.screenwritingexpo.com/

10 Ellroy has written screenplays for half a dozen of his own novels including the very successful *L.A. Confidential* (1997); Connelly has written for film and television, worked as an executive producer for television, and appeared as himself in several television shows; Crais has written extensively for television cop shows including *Miami Vice, Cagney & Lacey*, and *Hill Street Blues*; and Parker wrote a television show from his novel *Laguna Heat*. The intertwined fiction, screenplays, and journalism of Joan Didion and John Gregory Dunne are an impressive recent example of the possibilities of this industrial literature.

11 Bukowski, *Hollywood* (Santa Rosa: Black Sparrow Press, 1997); the film was *Barfly* (Barbet Schroeder, 1987).

12 *Los Angeles* (Harmondsworth: Penguin, 1990) 23.

13 Charles A. Stoddard, cit., Carey McWilliams [1946], *Southern California: An Island on the Land* (Salt Lake City: Peregrine Smith, 1973) 314.

14 McWilliams, *Southern California,* 315.

15 Figures from Paul Ong and Evelyn Blumberg, "Income and Racial Inequality in Los Angeles," in Soja and Scott, eds., *The City*, 323–24; and Soja, *Thirdspace*, p. 226. Figures for Los Angeles County are essentially the same: in 2000, Hispanics comprised 46%, Anglos 32%, Blacks 9%, and Asians 13%; see *Sprawl Hits the Wall: Confronting the Realities of Metropolitan Los Angeles* (Los Angeles: Southern California Studies Center, University of Southern California, 2001) 7. This and earlier immigration is directly represented in a novelistic subgenre that might be called the "coming to Los Angeles *bildungsroman*": Examples include Cynthia Kadohata, *The Floating World* (New York, N.Y.: Viking, 1989), Brian Ascalon Roley, *American Son* (New York: Norton, 2001) and Aimee Phan, *We Should Never Meet* (New York: St. Martin's Press, 2004) for recent Japanese, Pilipino, and Vietnamese immigrants respectively, with Kim Ronyoung's *Clay Walls* (Sag Harbor, NY: Permanent Press, 1986) a version constructed on Korean immigration in the 1920s. The best account of recent ethnic literature in Los Angeles is Julian Murphet, *Literature and Race in Los Angeles* (Cambridge: Cambridge University Press, 2001).

16 For an overview of these communities formed around other non-industrial cultural practices, see David E. James, ed., *The Sons and Daughters of Los: Culture and Community in L.A.*, (Philadelphia: Temple University Press, 2003).

17 New York: New American Library, 1967.

18 Albuquerque, New Mexico: West End Press, 1989. All three had recently published chapbooks of their own with the same press (before it relocated from Los Angeles to Albuquerque): Michelle T. Clinton, *High Blood/Pressure* (Los Angeles: West

End Press, 1986). Naomi Quiñonez, *Sueño de colibrí/Hummingbird Dream* (Los Angeles: West End Press, 1985), and Sesshu Foster, *Angry Days* (Los Angeles: West End Press, 1987). Foster has continued to write poetry and fiction of starting originality, creating a distinctively working-class aesthetic across his joint Japanese- and Mexican American heritage, and firmly anchored in the spatiality of East Los Angeles; see especially *City Terrace: A Field Manual* (New York: Kaya Production, 1996) and *Atomik Aztex* (San Francisco: City Lights Publishers, 2005).

19   Ulin's *Writing Los Angeles* manifests the former impulse while Messerli's *Intersections*, the latter. Of the twenty eight poets in *Intersections*, only three were people of color, though nine were women; yet, of the eight people pictured on the cover, four were women and two African American. The emergence of minority poetry was accompanied by a boom of neo-noir industrial fiction featuring minority protagonists, especially ethnic, to varying degrees displaced from the hegemony that earlier noir attempted to preserve. The genre was perhaps initiated in *Fadeout* (1970), the first of the Dave Brandstetter novels featuring a gay detective by Joseph Hansen, also an important poet. Of more recent minority or non-mainstream noirish novelists, particularly interesting are Gordon DeMarco, Janet Fitch, Rochelle Krich, Gary Phillips, Nina Revoyr, Nancy Taylor Rosenberg, and Pamela L. Woods; none of these have written for the cinema, though Fitch's novel, *White Oleander* and Krich's *Where's Mommy Now?* have been filmed. Pamela L. Woods "Charlotte Justice" novels are especially noteworthy for their precise descriptions of actual streets and buildings (her website even has photographs of them juxtaposed with relevant excerpts: see http://woodsontheweb.com/, and for their inversions of generic stereotypes; Justice is a woman detective, from an upper middle class black Los Angeles family, who is torn between the racism and corruption of her fellow officers and her own commitment to the LAPD. Her *Stormy Justice* (New York: Norton, 2001) is set specifically in Hollywood and has numerous references to cinema and the roles of African Americans in the industry. None of Sue Grafton's very successful Kinsey Millhone detective novels, set in nearby Santa Barbara but containing recurrent visits to Los Angeles, has been filmed, but she has written and produced extensively for television.

20   Douglas Messerli, "Intersections: Innovative Poetry in Southern California," introduction to Messerli, ed., *Intersections* 7.

21   For a pioneering account of the way small press publishers have constructed communities of poets in Los Angeles, see William Mohr, "Backlit: Los Angeles and the West Coast Poetry Renaissance" (Ph.D. diss., University of California at San Diego, 2004). See also his "from *Rear Projections*," *The New Review of Literature* 3.1 (October 2005): 29–50.

22 Vangelisti, *L.A. Exiles* 13.

23 *Gunga Din Highway* (Minneapolis: Coffee House Press, 1994). On Chin and the relation between ethnic identity and the mass media in Asian American writing in Los Angeles, see David E. James, "Tradition and the Movies: The Asian American Avant-Garde in Los Angeles," *Journal of Asian American Studies* 2.2 (June 1999): 157–180.

24 See Chin, Frank, Jeffrey Chan, Lawson Fusao Inada, and Shawn H. Wong. "Fifty Years of Our Whole Voice: An Introduction to Chinese and Japanese American Literatures," in Frank Chin, Jeffrey Chan, Lawson Fusao Inada, and Shawn H. Wong, eds., *The Big Aiiieeeee!: An Anthology of Asian American Writers* (New York: Mentor, 1991) xii.

25 See Susan Koshy, "The Fiction of Asian American Literature," *Yale Journal of Criticism* 9.2 (1996): 315–346 and Lisa Lowe, "Heterogeneity, Hybridity, Multiplicity: Asian American Differences" in her *Immigrant Acts: On Asian American Cultural Politics* (Durham: Duke University Press, 1996).

26 See, for example, Amy Uyematsu, *30 Miles From J-Town* (Brownsville, Or.: Story Line Press, 1992) and Russell Leong, *Country of Dreams and Dust* (Los Angeles; West End Press, 1994).

27 Kubernik's enormously important spoken word recordings include *Voices of the Angels* (Torrance, Ca: Freeway Records, 1982), *English as a Second Language* (Torrance, Ca: Freeway Records, 1983), *Neighborhood Rhythms* (Torrance, Ca: Freeway Records, 1983), Michael C. Ford, *Language Commando* (Lawndale, Ca: New Alliance Records, 1986), Michael C. Ford, *Motel Café* (Los Angeles: Blue Yonder Sounds, 1986), *Black Angels: Michelle T. Clinton and Wanda Coleman* (Lawndale, Ca: New Alliance Records, 1988), *Hollyword* (Lawndale, Ca: New Alliance Records, 1991), *Black & Tan Club* (Lawndale, Ca: New Alliance Records, 1991), Wanda Coleman, *High Priestess of Word* (Venice, Ca: New Alliance Records, 1990), *JazzSpeak* (Lawndale, Ca: New Alliance Records, 1991), and Bill Mohr *Vehemence* (Lawndale, Ca: New Alliance Records, 1993).

28 On the various graffiti writing communities, see Rubén Martinez, "Going Up in L.A.," in Ulin, ed., *Writing Los Angeles* 735–749.

29 On punk poetry in Los Angeles, see David E. James, "Poetry/Punk/Production: Some Postmodern Writing in L.A," *Power Misses: Essays Across (Un)Popular Culture* (London: Verso Books, 1996) 191–214.

30 See Webb, *Stand Up Poetry*.

31 The coincidence of class and ethnic segregation was especially acute in South Central Los Angeles, the area where blacks had historically concentrated but which was increasingly occupied by refugees and illegal immigrants from Latin

America. By 1979, the poverty rate in Los Angeles was 1% higher than the national average, and a decade later 15% of the nation's poor lived in the city. See Ong and Blumberg, "Income and Racial Inequality" 322–23.

32 See George J., Borjas, *Heaven's Door: Immigration Policy and the American Economy* (Princeton, N.J.: Princeton University Press, 1999) and George J. Borjas and Lawrence F. Katz, "The Evolution of the Mexican-Born Workforce in the United States (Working Paper, March 2006). Thus, for example, one of the great successes of the recent labor movement in Los Angeles has been the Service Employees International Union (SEIU)'s organization of janitors, who are now largely Mexican immigrants; celebrations of their very important achievement forget that fifteen years ago the then-largely Black janitors' union was destroyed by union busting by Mexican immigrants. On hate crimes by Latinos against Blacks, see, for example, Joe Mozingo, "Highland Park Gang Trial Paints a Portrait of Hate," *Los Angeles Times* 25 July 2006: B1.

33 See Nancy Cleland, "L.A. Area Going to Extremes as the Middle Class Shrinks," *Los Angeles Times* 23 July 2006: B1, 18–19.

34 Paul Vangelisti, "Why I am a Socialist," *Invisible City* 1 (1971): 1–2.

© RMcN

PAUL VANGELISTI | *Memory and Daily Life*
in The Invisible City

I must begin by mentioning the debt of gratitude I owe the Parisian poet Mohammed Dib, who consistently made me aware that Los Angeles was indeed the Invisible City, borrowing from me, as it were, the title of my literary magazine, *Invisible City*, which I edited with John McBride from 1971–1982. During his stay in Los Angeles in 1974, Dib would often smile his capricious, little smile and ask, as the afternoon began to cool, if it weren't time to set off in my Datsun sedan and visit our invisible city, so that we may begin to add to it our own *"petites histoires."* Twenty-five years later, shortly before his death, we collaborated on a *"roman en vers,"* *L.A. Trip*, where he used the words *Invisible City*, always in italics, prominently throughout the work.

Poetry for me, then, issues from the invisible city, the big nowhere that is Los Angeles. Ours is a city of "theatrical impermanence," as Christopher Isherwood called it, the home of tautological architecture, where hot dog and hamburger and donut stands take on the shape of hot dogs and hamburgers and donuts, where at any given time only a little more than one-third of the populations has lived there more than five years. Los Angeles is blessed, in Tennessee Williams' words, with "wonderful rocking horse weather," and a curious light so mesmerizing that, as Orson Welles once noted, "You sit down, you're twenty-five, and when you get up, you're sixty-two." It functions, according to the poet Thomas McGrath, as the "Asia Minor of the intellect," a place where, in the immortal words of the legendary producer Irving Thalberg (namesake for the Academy's Oscar for "life-time achievement"), the writer is no less than "a necessary evil." Los Angeles is also a place that has afforded writers and artists, to borrow a phrase from long-time resident Igor Stravinsky, "splendid isolation." Memory in so willfully forgetful a place is critical, defining an almost palpable dimension of daily life which is all the more vivid in contrast to the perpetual elsewhere that best describes one's writing practice there.

Let me begin by describing two compositional devices that I have relied on to embody in my work the urge to remember. The first of these is the fiction or novel-in-verse, of which I have written three in the last twenty years. In two of these long poems, "Villa" and "Earthly Science," the epistolary is at the heart not only of personal recollection but of a more general attempt at historical understanding.

Written from 1983–1986, "Villa" is made up of thirty-three letters from one Gaius Paullus Lunatus, a courtier at Hadrian's Villa outside Rome, sent to friends over a three-year period at the end of Hadrian's reign, 136–138 AD. Lunatus disappears in the days immediately following the Emperor's death. His friend, Gaius Suetonius Tranquillus (AKA the historian Suetonius, author of *Lives of the Twelve Caesars* and other even more famous works which do not survive), collects the letters from their recipients – friends, lovers, business associates and family – as testimony to the lost Lunatus and the magnificent Villa constructed by Hadrian and abandoned after his death. Suetonius also writes a preface to the thirty-three letters, explaining his editorial methodology beginning with these remarks:

My dismissal and distance from the imperial court first made me safeguard his Tiburtine missives. Of late I have discovered that, happily, others had done the same. The assembled memoranda may now open windows, however narrow, where otherwise would be a wall. A chronicle they are not, though here they follow chronologically.

"Earthly Science," which I worked on from 1993–1997, claims to be derived from copies of original letters composed, circa 1370, by an unnamed cleric for one Caterina Benincasa, later known as Saint Catherine of Siena. Again thirty-three in number, they were presumably written by Catherine's first confessor, of whom little if anything is known, rather than her second and more celebrated cleric, Raymond of Capua, who eventually wrote her hagiography and parlayed this notoriety into becoming the head of the Dominican order. "Earthly Science" gets its title from the Earth Sciences Department at Melbourne Polytechnic High School, where the remote descendant of the purported letter writer, one Gianni V., had worked as a custodian before retiring to live six-months of the year in his native city of Modena. There, as the story goes, I met him at the bar we both frequented. The letters were left to Gianni V. in 1965, by an aunt who was a nun and had died in a convent near Bologna. In "Earthly Science," as yet unpublished in its entirety, I am listed as the editor and translator of the collection. As editor and translator, I also wrote a brief introduction divided into three parts, "Provenance," "Translation," and "The Original," which I conclude in the following way: "There are dogs, in Ovid, who bite the air. I choose my own tongue as opponent."

I think it is worth noting that in both "Villa" and "Earthly Science" the fictive philological or historical method is a vital component. How the letters came to us, to whom they were written, who edited or translated them, who was part of a larger circle of recipients, and many other such questions regarding their historical identity are indeed critical. They help create that patina of time past, recalled and forgotten, that is an essential ingredient of one of the properties of literature most dear to me, what Samuel Johnson termed the "reek of the human." Later in this talk, I will more explicitly describe how for me language and the world collide in the memory of daily life.

The third fiction-in-verse, "Gold Mountain," written between 1997–1998, is set in 1897 Los Angeles, and was spurred by the accidental unearthing of a late-nineteenth century brothel, while sinking a foundation for a new parking structure on Alameda Street alongside Union Station, in the old historical center of the city. Having seen the item in the *Los Angeles Times*, I immediately went down to the site, not far from my house, and was quite moved in viewing the brick ruins of a very large establishment, conveniently near the train station, with over a hundred rooms or 6 × 10 foot "cribs," where the women or, in some cases girls, lived and worked. There didn't seem to be much local interest in the site, except for one team of archeologists from California State Polytechnic in San Luis Obispo, some two-hundred miles to the north of Los Angeles, who received a one-month clearance to dig before the garage foundation would be poured and this part of Los Angeles's past sealed forever. Their findings were fascinating, giving us a quite detailed picture of these lost lives which were so central to the early days of the city and which would be in no way commemorated in the city's incessant mania toward boosterism, and a most shameful rewriting of history.

After researching the subject of prostitution in early Los Angeles and the American West, I was particularly struck by the assessment that in frontier towns of the 1870s and '80s, at least 40% of the women were or had been prostitutes, and so I began "Gold Mountain." The poem is made up of six books, with a company of five prostitutes, ages fifteen to thirty, who deliver monologues in their own dialects. One of them, the only Anglo woman in the group, writes letters; the others speak in their own voices and forms of English, regardless of how non-standard those might be. This was the first and only time in my writing that I have tried to speak through the persona of a woman but I could not ignore my concern with these "mothers of our country." As historian W.W. Robinson makes a point of reminding us in his study of prostitution in the formative years of Los Angeles, *Tarnished Angels* (1961): "All these sights are recalled by still-living ex-judges, ex-lawyers, ex-officials, and ex-businessmen, Angelenos of distinction and of excellent memory."

The other compositional device I would mention, if only briefly, is the alphabet poem. Five alphabets or abcedariums were written between 1986 and 1997, and were collected in the book *Alphabets* (1999), while two more, "Days Shadows Pass" and "Alabaster," were completed in 2003 and 2005, respectively. The pieces are composed in either twenty-six stanzas, as with my first two "Los Alephs" and "Alephs Again," or in twenty-six sections or poem sequences, as with the remaining five alphabets ("Rhum" is a double alphabet of 52 parts with each section a fourteen line poem). The confines of their common structure allows for a recording of daily life, as well as social history, as there are friends, family and other writers and artists who appear within, or perhaps better, on the stage of the various letter forms. "The Simple Life" (1993) is a bestiary, each poem bearing the name of an animal, and each also dedicated to a friend, fellow artist or member of my family. In "A Life" (1991), the poems are meditations on particular letters, bearing the names of the Semitic letter form that were the origin of the particular modern Roman letters in question. The poems trace, among other things, how a letter ventured from the Phoenician alphabet to Greek to Latin to our English of today, with many unexpected stops along the way. In the alphabet of "Days Shadows Pass," each of the twenty-six lines of the twenty-six poems in the sequence is instead defined by absence or loss; for instance, the first line of each is missing the letter *a*, the second line the letter *b* and so forth.

There is nothing more ordinary, mundane and material to the practice of writing as the alphabet; also there is not a technology as fundamentally telling to the human condition, especially in such a dislocated environment as Los Angeles. In short, these alphabets afford a meditative structure that is at once personal and public, temporary and historical, in which to house my verse. Here, in number 15 of "Days Shadows Pass," the 26-line poem begins by taking stock of yet another day, of tending to the ordinary motion of life beyond the desk, where the poet watches and waits for something no more uncommon than the next line dictated by the next missing letter of the alphabet:

Orchid or mockingbird or plenty plenty
heat and smell of jasmine or squeaky hummer,
a trilling something or other like an alarm
gone berserk in the trees across the way.
August full blown noon and blinding as
the sound of mailman setting his emergency
on the hill outside beyond the fenced-in
garden. Number O audacious number
show your melody doubled as pale fate
genuine and large or largely motion.

I now shift to a description of a poetic of daily life, where *house* or *house* is indeed the operative term. Given the constant embarrassment of survival, I use daily life or the quotidian (more often than not in a mock heroic manner) to find common forms to supplant some of the social functions of narrative. In supplanting or, more ingenuously, trying to seduce narrative, one wishes to accommodate that most wicked and happy of creatures – time. Time and place operate curiously in the daily and often dull ineptitude of a grammar that might describe such a fictive utility as Los Angeles. Time, for instance, as briefly noted at the start of this talk, may function as a property of light, a perpetual present or "timelessness" in close relationship to the peculiarly isolate and meditative light that is the single most distinguishing characteristic of our city. "Lots and lots of light – and no shadows," notes artist Robert Irwin, "really peculiar, almost dreamlike."

Inhabiting this light, then, is the citizen who recently, near the corner of Sunset and Alvarado, was shouting at the rush hour traffic: "What the fuck are you looking at?" or, no less enthusiastically, "What the hell are you doing here *you*?" (The same place, parenthetically, where Mohammed Dib set his poem from *L.A. Trip*, "Carrefour Sunset et Alvarado.") Or there was the barefoot stranger a few years ago, bearing a mop and empty bucket across Hollywood Boulevard, pausing in the crosswalk in front of my car to say that he knew me and knew what I was doing there.

I am suggesting that a preoccupation with our daily bread is a poet's attempt to ground his or her work if not exactly in some form of realism, at least in a realistic attitude or position within this wacky environment. Lacking the public occasion and certainly the public form for serious literature – museums and other educational and public institutions in our city are hardly more than specimen boxes in today's cultural marketplace – some poets instinctively employ the daily to create a context for their work, social, dramatic or otherwise. In a city where the image is considered truthful, and entrepreneurs the likes of (fill in the name of whatever current pop culture boss) are discussed in university and college classrooms as creative geniuses, a poet may look to his or her own isolate daily life to fashion a background against which language may be given room for serious play.

The notion of serious play is critical here. Not only the sense of play as action, movement or use, as in the play of imagination or the play of light on a leaf or wall, but the idea of play taken from mechanics, that is, the space for varied movement, as in the play in a wheel or rope. What daily life appears to offer is a sense of a larger context, the high and low of subject Whitman called for, in 1855, when he said that the poem must be "democratic and have vistas." Formally, the use of daily life as a marker and even as an object of contemplation insures an immediate though something less than personal look at the personal, engaging a social and linguistic register more outwardly inclusive than with subjects demanding, for instance, a cultural or historical background. Also, as mentioned earlier, the quotidian implies the broader and more varied perspective of comedy, as opposed to a more exclusive, tragic vision. Again, in formal terms, many varied techniques and languages may be deployed to suggest the passage of time which characterizes living day to day.

Experience, then, that great leveler, is at the heart of our discussion. The illusion of daily life allowed poets as temperamentally disparate as Ezra Pound, Marianne Moore, Wallace Stevens and Jack Spicer to establish a critical and progressive realism in their poetry. Pound's depiction of the daily business of writing (from classical China, Rome, the Renaissance courts, to the U.S. Senate and ultimately military prison and the asylum), Moore's use of magazines and newspapers in her collages, Stevens' subjecting of mundane physical objects to lyrical and epistemological scrutiny, Spicer's para-surrealistic constructions of everyday speech events, all find a common impulse to produce the kind of poetic language they envisioned reality speaking through them. Even at the root of Ezra Pound's and T.S. Eliot's grudging acceptance of Walt Whitman and his populist excesses is their understanding, as both poets set out to attempt longer work, of the realistic nuance Whitman achieved by means of his varied linguistic register.

A cautionary note here. Experience is indeed a great and treacherous leveler, especially for a nation such as ours whose dominant philosophical and ideological bent is pragmatism. Associated with, though fundamentally corrupting to this critical realism, has been a tendency in twentieth-century Anglo-American writing toward an internalized and Puritanical response to experience, treating poetry in particular, with its precarious social demarcation, as little more than a signature of individual consciousness – what may be going on inside the mind of the writer. Through a series of ostensibly radical operations, more often than not enshrining the writing process itself, poetry is made, in Gertrude Stein's words, to "consist of an exact reproduction of outer or inner reality." Thus experience, which has the propensity to challenge, threaten, keep us, in Kenneth Burke's phrase, "from becoming hopelessly ourselves," is instead conflated with one of the most pragmatic and reductive of experiences, the mental process of writing a poem.

What is indeed treacherous about the process of writing as subject is the false or naive realism engendered within the poet and, more lamentably, the audience called upon to accept this particular illusion. In this fool's purgatory of creativity, fact replaces event, information takes the place of interpretation, a mental state is mistaken for imagination, studied irrelevance for ideology, and so on. It is a curiously post-impressionistic paradigm, as if what the artist or poet considers while making art imbues the work with authenticity, relevance or whatever claim to objectivity locates the writing outside of its own frame of reference. Even worse, if the process has the relentless conviction of our daily lives.

The tug of this mental cinema, producing what Gilbert Sorrentino calls the "cliché in one swift image," can be difficult for all of us to resist. It is a mal-adjustment in our perception of the daily world all too often conditioned by the so-called creative process. Regardless of its daily process-driven impulse, what results is a kind of poetic speech that is anything but realistic, in any truly critical sense, or even musical for that matter. It becomes, in Pier Paolo Pasolini's words, an "esperanto," born out of the institutional need to deny language as the fruit of contradictory centuries, to deny the mystery of its wealth, by those who wish, as Pasolini writes, "to reduce man to their purity, who are chaos!"

Let us come back, then, to the notion of play and daily life. My reservations arise from practices that have tried to define the quotidian pragmatically, with process posing as some sort of realism, instead of placing the quotidian in the larger, more reckless and dynamic context of history, as I suggested earlier in my practice of composing verse-fictions or even alphabet poems. Thus, examining daily life by means of one of these fictive or philological techniques, the poet may step momentarily outside the poem, to incite a kind of double focus *on* and *in* the path of experience, while emphasizing that both may become fundamentally altered by the encounter. This tension is at the heart of poetic utterance, as it unfolds in the conclusion to the poem "Quotidian," the seventeenth section of my recently completed sequence "Alabaster":

Time seems what used to be lost in appetite not silence,
uncertain that light upholds things and things like birdsong
vastly usual above the flat tar roofs nearing noontime.
Wren variously hits two or three notes in the willow.
Expect word that there is no wren only a little boat
yaring expertly into the wind beyond the train station's
zesty yapping at all that hard freight once or twice in sleep.

Or, in further placing this collision of poetry and daily life, we may go all the way back to 1920's San Francisco, in the Dashiell Hammett story "Too Many Have Lived," where we find another appearance of Sam Spade, questioning the wife of a poet who has gone missing. "Spade scowled thoughtfully at the floor, asked, 'What did he do before he started not making a living writing poetry?'"

"Anything – sold vacuum cleaners, hoboed, went to sea, dealt blackjack, railroaded, canning houses, lumber camps, carnivals, worked on a newspaper – anything."

Daily life may be a useful, even dynamic invention if it drives the poet out of his mind, if only momentarily, and into the poem.

I have lived in Los Angeles for thirty-eight years, and find myself writing in a way that is necessarily both absent and present. Present in my passion for memory and a craft felt perhaps no more intimately than in such "splendid isolation," to repeat Stravinsky's phrase. Absent from the phony history, the boosterism, the evermore insidious banality of the entertainment industry or what most familiarly in this town is called "the Business." Finally, one can't help wondering if the memory of daily life itself, as a token of this habitually unfinished elsewhere, might not be one of the few oppositions a writer these days can muster.

© RMcN

CHRISTOPHE FIAT | *ESCAPE*

On John Carpenter

In 1981, the movie
Escape from New York
Translated in French as
New York 1997
Is a big step forward
For John Carpenter
Who just signed a second contract
For seven million dollars
With the Avco Embassy
production company.
Then John Carpenter
Works on another script written
In the mid-'70s
During Watergate.
John Carpenter is finally able
To think big
With this script
But the seven million dollar budget
Is a ridiculous amount
Considering the ambitions
Of the movie *Escape From New York*
Translated in French as
New York 1997
Which is a dark, futuristic movie
With a quirky sense of humor.

Indeed, John Carpenter
Wants to transform
The Manhattan peninsula
Into a high-security prison
With the Statue of Liberty
As a watch tower.

But John Carpenter
Can only shoot
Two days max
In New York
Because the city does not like
The project.
So, John Carpenter
Also shoots in Saint Louis
Missouri
And in Los Angeles
The set designer
Whose name is Joe Alves
And the team from the studios in charge of
Special effects
Do a wonderful job
To make us believe
That the movie really
Takes place in New York.
The first moments
Of *Escape From New York*
Translated in French as
New York 1997
Sum up the historical situation
Of an America plagued by facism
Through a voice over
And through suggestive inter titles.
The conciseness of the script

Which says far more
Than it shows
Forces John Carpenter
To shoot the first scenes
As long sequence shots.
Which leads to an efficient, sober
Spatial positioning of the most impressive
Monuments of the city
Of New York.
This way the audience
Is settled into
The familiar context
Of the city of New York City
NO DOUBT
WE ARE REALLY
IN NEW YORK NO DOUBT.

But *Escape From New York*
Translated in French as
New York 1997
Is not only a fable
On the future of the United States
But also a political movie
On fascism.
So in order to
Crystallize his doubts
And develop his hopes,
John Carpenter creates the character
Of Snake Plissken
Who becomes over the years
The emblematic figure
Of his filmmaking!
To create Snake Plissken
John Carpenter draws his inspiration

From a decorated war hero
Who became a gangster.
Snake Plissken has
A snake-shaped tattoo
On his belly
And he resists
All forms of authority.
So, Snake Plissken
Is a sociopath
Who loves total
Freedom
Because he does not like
To be told what to do
Or what not to do.
Snake Plissken
Who lives in a dangerous world
Is thus nicknamed
In a pithy turn of phrase:
"The man who wants to live 60 seconds more."

John Carpenter chooses
Ken Russel to play
The part of Snake Plissken
"Violent! Snake Plissken is violent!"
Says Ken Russel.
"Nihilistic! Snake Plissken is nihilistic!"
Says Ken Russel.
"Killer! Snake Plissken kills to survive"
Says Ken Russel
"One-eyed! Snake Plissken is one-eyed!"
Says Ken Russel
NO DOUBT
WE ARE REALLY
IN NEW YORK NO DOUBT

And it is the most violent place
In the United States!
So the character
Of Snake Plissken
Who becomes over the years
The emblematic figure
Of John Carpenter's filmmaking
Is an anti-hero
Who only reveals himself
In perilous situations
Faced with the adversity of a fascist society.

So since the beginning of the movie
Escape From New York
Translated in French as
New York 1997,
Snake Plissken, the anti-hero
Is shown in a position
Of weakness, handcuffed
And incapable
Of negociating the situation.
So policemen
Inject deadly capsules
Into his the blood
To force him to find
The president of the United States
Whose plane crashed
In the Manhattan peninsula
Which has become a high security
Prison.

In 1994, the movie
Escape From Los Angeles
Translated in French as

Los Angeles 2013
Is also a big step forward
For John Carpenter who can
Make his first
American blockbuster.
So he signs
A contract for 50 million dollars
With Paramount Studios to shoot
The sequel of the adventures
Of Snake Plissken.
John Carpenter's goal
Is to introduce
Snake Plissken
To the general public.
John Carpenter
Writes the script at a time
When Los Angeles has just been struck
By natural disasters
(Earthquake)
And social strife
(Riots)
So shot after shot,
John Carpenter,
Is literally going to mould
The matrix movie
Escape From New York
Translated in French as
New York 1997
By presenting
As the introduction
The political background
(Fascist America)
The presentation of the character
Of Snake Plissken

Snake Plissken's mission
But also by constantly returning to
The narrative principles
Of *Escape From New York*
Translated in French as
From New York 1997
But adjusting them
To this new set
On the West coast.
NO DOUBT
WE ARE IN LOS ANGELES NO DOUBT.

TWENTY YEARS HAVE PASSED
BUT SNAKE PLISSKEN
HAS NOT CHANGED A BIT
AND THE MOST INCURABLE
OF THE SOCIOPATHS
WHO SAVED
THE PRESIDENT OF THE UNITED STATES
IN 1997 IN NEW YORK
MUST FIND IN LOS ANGELES IN 2013
A BLACK BOX
THAT WILL ALLOW THE NEW
PRESIDENT OF THE UNITED STATES
TO CONTROL ALL
ELECTRONIC SYSTEMS
AND THUS WIN HIS WAR
AGAINST THE THIRD WORLD.
SO SNAKE PLISSKEN
HAS TO GET THE BLACK BOX
FROM A REVOLUTIONARY
WHO ALSO INTENDS
TO HAVE THE WORLD AT HIS MERCY.

So unlike New York,
Los Angeles is not
A high security prison
But the only land of freedom
In an America
Plagued by fascism.
Snake Plissken says that Los Angeles
Is a "dark paradise."
So John Carpenter
Pushing the satire
Of the film *Escape From New York*
Translated in French as
New York 1997
Transforms all the failings
Of Californian culture
Into hitherto imperceptible
Dangers:
Basketball, cosmetic surgery,
Surfing are becoming life-and-death issues
For Snake Plissken.
And while he is at it,
John Carpenter takes the opportunity
To drown a few icons
Of the West Coast
Like in the underwater scene
Where Snake Plissken
Gets to Los Angeles
In a submarine and crosses
The ruins of Universal Studios
On his way.
NO DOUBT
WE ARE IN LOS ANGELES NO DOUBT.

John Carpenter says that a society
Crushed by fascism
Is a society that abandons
Freedom for
Order and religion
And which deludes itself
With technology.
So at the beginning of the movie
Escape From Los Angeles
Translated in French as
Los Angeles 2013,
A voice lists
The rules to be followed in 2013:
No talking
No smoking
No littering
No eating red meat,
No religious choice,
No marrying
Without the consent
Of the American
Department of Health.
The smallest offence
Automatically results in
The permanent loss of citizenship.
So Snake Plissken's response
To these rules
Who is an anti-hero
Who does not like to be told
What to do or what not to do
Is: "Your rules are really beginning to annoy me!"

Translated by Béatrice Mousli

BILL KROHN | *Los Angeles in Cinema*

Los Angeles is the most photographed city in the world because Hollywood is here, and because most TV series are filmed here – or were until Canada became cheaper. But the city really became a character – became conscious of itself – only after the war, when classic examples of film noir like *The Big Sleep* and *Double Indemnity* limned a City of Night that had already been imagined for filmmakers by noir novelists like Raymond Chandler and James M. Cain.

In a Lonely Place, Kiss Me Deadly and *Sunset Boulevard* and their ilk are films about Los Angeles, and offer precious glimpses of the city as it was in the '40s and '50s: a dusty, sun-dappled bungalow hiding from the heat behind venetian blinds, a supermarket in Glendale, a real drugstore where Rudolph Mate staged a shootout in *Union Station*. That identity still clings to the city of *Chinatown, L.A. Confidential, Whatever Happened to Baby Jane, The Long Goodbye, Barton Fink, Who Framed Roger Rabbit, Collateral, Boyz in the Hood, Training Day, American Gigolo, Heat, Blade Runner, Terminator 1* and *2, Pulp Fiction* and *Mulholland Drive*.

There is another genre specific to Los Angeles, invented by Robert Altman: the multi-character ensemble film, which reflects the ethnic and economic balkanization of the city, with immigrants clustered in neighborhoods where English is not spoken, and no homeless bums looking into the window of pricey Beverly Hills stores – something that is quite possible even today in Manhattan, for example. *Magnolia, Short Cuts* and *Crash* are fables – people may say the things we hear in *Crash* to themselves in the privacy of their cars; they don't say them

177

out loud – but their structure is as much "about" Los Angeles as the chiaroscuro of all those postwar film noirs.

The first Altman ensemble was *Nashville*, in which the country music capital was really a metaphor: denizens of Hollywood disguised as citizens of Nashville enacting a scenario at once prophetic (Pauline Kael's famous review of the film spoke of the fusion of fundamentalism and celebrity culture, the two forces dominating American culture today) and secretly retrospective. The political assassination that kills the wrong person at the end really happened on Hollywood's doorstep in June of 1968, and the target was not a displaced one. It is no accident that Emilio Estevez's *Bobby*, the first Hollywood film that directly confronts the memory of RFK's assassination, is a homage to *Nashville*.

Here are ten Los Angeles films I recommend for natives and visitors alike:

- *Kiss Me Deadly* (1955), in many ways the ultimate L.A. film, begins with a naked woman running in a car's headlights and ends with a mushroom cloud. In between, nothing resembling a human being crosses the path of Mike Hammer, Mickey Spillane's detective hero, who is transformed by the genius of A.I. Bezzerides (script) and Robert Aldrich (direction) into a crypto-fascist with a pad right out of *Playboy*.
- *The Graduate* (1967) captures the sun-drenched, slick surfaces of Los Angeles in the late '60s, when "plastic" was still the magic word in some quarters, but the sulfurous hints of incest from the days of Ross MacDonald and Raymond Chandler seem to linger like an ancestral curse over the city's bourgeoisie, only to be vanquished by youthful idealism at the end.
- *The Party* (1968) is a Jacques Tati homage set in a rich producer's luxurious home that serves as a metaphor for Hollywood: the film industry. Through an impressively orchestrated crescendoing series of sight gags, the place is dismantled in the course of a cocktail party by a band of miscreants representing youth culture,

Europe and the Third World (the Indian party crasher played by Peter Sellers). Blake Edwards' masterpiece saw what was going to happen to Hollywood in the '70s and rejoiced in it.

- *Model Shop* (1968) is an L.A. film that only a European could have made. Empowered by his Oscar for *Umbrellas of Cherbourg*, Jacques Demy freely filmed Los Angeles in the Age of Aquarius as a grid where chance meetings – the hero meets the heroine of Demy's *Lola* working in a sleazy photo joint – are programmed by the geometry of the city.

- *Lions Love* (1969) was the film Demy's wife Agnes Varda was making at the same time. Entirely improvised by a cast on LSD, led by the incomparable Viva, it is the only film ever made that accurately captures the weird Chinese box structure of certain LSD experiences. The murders of RFK and Andy Warhol appear on television – one of those boxes.

- *L.A. 2017* (1971), a hard-to-find television film directed by a very young Steven Spielberg, transforms an episode of the Los Angeles-based series *Name of the Game* into a dystopian science fiction parable by Philip Wylie about a future L.A. shaped by overpopulation and environmental catastrophes: *Blade Runner avant la lettre*.

- *Chinatown* (1974) is in some ways a remake of *Vertigo*, Hitchcock's hymn to L.A.'s sister city by the Bay. But whereas Hitchcock still had all those landmarks from another era to film in the '50s, by 1974 Roman Polanski had to go to the poor neighborhoods to find architecture of the '20s and '30s that was still standing. On the other hand, the quality of the light he and cameraman captured, which channels all the film's connotations of luxury and decadence, hadn't changed since Billy Wilder revealed it in *Double Indemnity*.

- *Who Framed Roger Rabbit* (1988) replaces Chinatown with Toon Town, and uses the technologically awesome wedding of 'toons and humans to evoke a symbol of L.A.'s vanished past: the Red Car that went everywhere before freeways and car culture devoured the city in the 1950s.

- *Collateral* (2004) has the distinction of being one of the few Los Angeles films that Thom Andersen, the acerbic author of *Los Angeles Plays Itself*, credits with getting the city right. Michael Mann used high-definition cameras to capture something never seen before in a film: the glow of the city's lights reflected off the perpetual cloud cover at night. Jamie Foxx's wandering taxi takes us to several specimens of the private worlds that make up L.A. by night or day.
- *Kiss Kiss, Bang Bang* (2005), Shane Black's postmodern homage to L.A., Chandler and film noir, features a pair of unlikely partners – a burglar-turned-actor played by Robert Downey, Jr., and an unabashedly homosexual private detective named Gay Perry (Val Kilmer) – who will not be replacing the *Lethal Weapon* team (also Black's creation) at the multiplex anytime soon. If you have ever eaten in a trendy L.A. restaurant, you have to love a film where Downey's offscreen voice introduces itself with a variation on the formula used by aspiring actors working as waiters: "I'm Charles. I'll be your narrator...."

JEAN-LOUP BOURGET | *Los Angeles in Film:*
A European View

Contemporary American cinema frequently offers us a striking image of Los Angeles, a case in point being *Crash* with its night scenes, constantly marauding cars, violent ethnic and social tensions, omnipresent violence (or at least threat of violence), not to mention verbal assault. While the film's fragmented form, like Altman's *Short Cuts* or Paul Thomas Anderson's *Magnolia* (set in the San Fernando Valley), can of course be a source of great intellectual and aesthetic pleasure, it also quite clearly reflects life in an enormous, sprawling, ill-defined, and centerless urban environment. To be sure, as in the case of other North American cities, the viewer can identify a downtown with a few skyscrapers providing a backdrop for narrowly-focused, "classic" dramatic action, but mainly she sees vacant lots, sprawling suburbs, a checkerboard or patchwork of communities, whose characteristic sprawl requires long car trips. The images offered by Helmholtz or Poincaré to explain non-Euclidian geometries (such as Riemann's) come to mind in this connection: flat fish living on the surface of a spherical world would only be capable of conceiving of a world in two dimensions. Come to think of it, this is a staple in cinematic representations of Los Angeles: it was already there in Alan Rudolph's *Welcome to L.A.*, in which a character (played by Geraldine Chapman) literally spends all her time driving on the freeway; and even love is fragmented, is itself patchwork-like, its only unifying feature being its very disparateness. We get the same urban (or suburban) feel – plasticity, malleability, *centerlessness*, lack of symmetry – in otherwise very different works: in "*neo-noirs*" like Michael Mann's

Collateral, where Tom Cruise, playing a melancholy killer an angel of death, seems a contemporary avatar of Alan Ladd in *Guns for Hire*; in gloomy road movies like Wim Wender's *Land of Plenty*; in stylish road movies like David Lynch's *Mulholland Drive* – not to mention innumerable action films and comedies depicting characters in hot pursuit of one another across a web of city freeways.

In the case of *Mulholland Drive* and many others, such as Curtis Hanson's *L.A. Confidential*, it is a glamorous or sordid Hollywood that is being described. (To tell the truth, it is more often a glamorous *and* sordid Hollywood, the luxury a facade barely concealing private drama and moral turpitude). This rather clichéd view belongs to a long tradition, marked notably by the three versions of *A Star is Born* (1937, 1954, 1976) – and even before that by Selznick and Cukor's *What Price Hollywood?* as well as Billy Wilder's *Sunset Boulevard* (more of which in due course) or *The Last Tycoon* by Elia Kazan.

A brief examination of the catalogues of the American Film Institute and their indexes turns up a number of places in Los Angeles where movies were shot on location in the 1930s and '40s: The Biltmore, which one sees in the first version of *A Star is Born* (directed by William Weltman in 1937) and which Harold Lloyd famously climbed in *Feet First* (1930); Grauman's Chinese Theater; Griffith Park, immortalized by the remark made by a producer: "A rock is a rock, and a tree is a tree. Shoot it in Griffith Park!"; more recently Griffith Park appeared with the same sort of anonymous ordinariness as the backdrop for *Short Cuts*; the Hollywood Bowl (in the aforementioned version of a *Star is Born* and in George Sidney's *Anchors Aweigh*); The Shrine (once the home of the Oscars); stadiums and railway stations (Union Station), university campuses (UCLA and USC), and even Chinatown (Josef von Sternberg's *The Shanghai Gesture*).

In his documentary, or rather his film essay *Los Angeles Plays Itself, Part One*, Thom Andersen revisits some of these places, so familiar to L.A. residents, not to mention the average cinema-goer: The Bradbury (featured in *D.O.A.* by Rudolph Maté, *Marlowe* by Paul Bogart, and Ridley Scott's *Blade Runner*), the Ennis house in the Hollywood

Hills, designed by Frank Lloyd Wright (*Female* by Michael Curtiz, *House on Haunted Hill* by William Castle, *Blade Runner*), the Lovell house, designed by Richard Neutra (*L.A. Confidential*), Grauman's Chinese Theatre, the Griffith Planetarium (*Rebel Without a Cause* by Nicholas Ray), the Bunker Hill neighborhood and its cable car (Robert Siodmak's *Criss Cross*, Douglas Sirk's *Shockproof* from a script by Samuel Fuller, *Kiss Me* by Robert Aldrich). Andersen points out that before it featured in Barry Levinson's *Bugsy*, *The Way We Were* by Sydney Pollack and *Blade Runner*, Union Station had appeared in *Union Station* by Rudolph Maté (1950), a film in which, despite the title, the action is not situated with any precision: if the name suggests Los Angeles, it is also evocative of New York and Chicago (because of its references to the El – or elevated light rail – and to its stockyards). In this case, it is clear that we are dealing with a work that partakes of the convention common to many *noir* thrillers, whose action is set in a composite city, a sort of Anytown, USA. On this point, it should be remembered that these real L.A. locations of course have been used of course to depict other places in the films in which they have appeared: thus The Shrine stood in for a New York theater in *King Kong* and scenes in Frank Capra's *Lost Horizon* were shot at LAX.

It is interesting to look more closely at the 1940s and the birth of *film noir*, which appears to me inextricable from the urban landscape of Los Angeles. Gangster films, from their beginnings to their heyday in the 1930s, tend to be set either in New York (from D.W. Griffith's 1912 *Musketeers of Pig Alley* on), or in Chicago (*Scarface* by Ben Hecht and Howard Hawks), in other words in clearly identifiable urban environments. Thus in *Scarface*, Tony Camonte (Paul Muni) goes to the Chicago Opera; William Wellman's *The Public Enemy* is also supposed to take place in Chicago, even if, as Thom Andersen points out, certain scenes filmed in Los Angeles seem a little too rural to be taking place in the capital of the Midwest. Most of these films were filmed indoors and not outdoors on location, with a few notable exceptions – Manhattan's Lower East Side with its Yiddish signs and fruit and vegetable stalls being one, featuring in both *Musketeers of Pig Alley* and memorably in *The Naked City* (1948) by Mark Hellinger and Jules Dassin (1948), which was almost entirely filmed on location outdoors in New York. But, in the 1940s, when the themes and aesthetic of what would come to be called *"film noir"* were leaving their mark on the whole criminal movie genre, there was a marked shift to setting the action in California: in San Francisco and Los Angeles.

San Francisco was the setting, partially or totally, for the plots of *The Maltese Falcon*, adapted by John Huston of Dashell Hammett's book and often cited as the prototype of the *film noir;* of *Dark Passage* by Delmer Daves reworking of David Goodis' work; of Frank Tuttle's *Hell on Frisco Bay*, from William P. McGivern's book; of *Lady from Shanghai* by Orson Welles, with its classic finale, filmed in San Francisco's Chinatown. San Francisco would remain a favored venue for Hollywood movies, a fact explained by the city's spectacular scenery (above all the Golden Gate Bridge, the steep hills, the streetcars) and the double exoticism of Chinatown and the city's Spanish connection, present in the city's name as well as the baroque architecture of the Mission district. Everyone knows these features from Peter Yates's *Bullitt* (1968), and above all from Hitchcock's *Vertigo* (1958), two films – coincidentally? – made by English filmmakers based in Hollywood.

To tell the truth, even if Hitchcock preferred the spectacular backdrop of Northern California in *Vertigo* (as well as *The Birds*, set in San Francisco and Bodega Bay), Los Angeles could easily have provided the same Hispanic exoticism, with the Andalusia-inspired architecture of Pasadena or the San Gabriel Mission replacing the Dolores Mission. What is more, whether it be frequent pronunciation of Los AnGeles with a hard "g" or the Spanish Revival houses (romanesque tiles, wrought iron, ceramics, eucalyptus trees), such as the one meticulously recreated to represent the villa of Phyllis Dietrichson (Barbara Stanwick) in Billy Wilder's *Double Indemnity*, there are traces of this exoticism everywhere.

Nevertheless, the novelty of the Los Angeles setting – a suburban rather than an urban environment, a place where it is pointless to seek a center, a place hemmed in by desert on one side and the

Pacific on the other – marks many *films noirs*: one has only to think of Michelangelo Antonioni's *Zabriskie Point* (1970) where the opposition of city and desert structures the action.

Also noteworthy are the opening scenes of a few archetypal *films noirs* set in Los Angeles, such as *The Big Sleep* by Howard Hawks or *The Brasher Doubloon* by John Brahm (two adaptations of novels by Raymond Chandler, a *hardboiled* author as associated with L.A. as Hammett is with San Francisco), *Sunset Boulevard* by Billy Wilder et even Chandler and Wilder's *Double Indemnity*. All of these stories begin with the main character (a private detective, penniless scriptwriter, insurance agent) visiting a luxury residence, for all the world resembling a lord's manor or mansion. The settings are all eclectic and, while there is no mistaking the sun-kissed Spanish Revival backdrop in *Double Indemnity* and the tropical greenhouse humidity that dominates in the home of Gereal Sternwood (*The Big Sleep*), the gothic, in various guises, pops up again and again. Malaise, disorientation, dead leaves blowing everywhere; the opening of *Brash Doubloon* explicitly pastiches a gothic movie, as does *Written on the Wind* by Sirk, a film taking place in Texas in an industrial and suburban setting that combines oil derricks and highways, a shapeless expanse not unlike Los Angeles. In this regard, the *noir genre* is part of the migration of the gothic from its imaginary beginnings in a Germany dreamt up in England and Ireland to the New World, where it initially became acclimatized in regions with their own very particular characters (New England and the South to be exact), before finding an ideal soil in California, especially Los Angeles.

Hence there is a sense of "disturbing strangeness," which as in Freud is in fact a "disturbing familiarity" in these films; not in the sense that they conjure up the shades of things once familiar, but rather because in them gothic anxiety is transmitted through the familiar, the banal, and the "100% American" forms of everyday existence. This was the reaction of European filmmakers (foreigners, artists and intellectuals from Berlin or Paris, disoriented by this centerless world) to their new Hollywood environment.

In reality, this feeling was not limited to the exiled community, since we find it in Hawk's *The Big Sleep*, or even more acutely in Robert Aldrich's work, a case in point being the unforgettable opening of *Kiss Me Deadly* on a road at night, where we are plunged into a mad, a topsy-turvy world; even the titles scroll by in reverse. Compare this to a photo by Cindy Sherman, *Untitled # 66,* from the series *Rear Screen Projections:* in the foreground of this work from 1980, which was featured in the recent *Cindy Sherman* exhibition at the *Jeu de paume* in Paris (May – September 2006), the artist, a blond wearing a jacket, is holding the handlebars of her bicycle while she turns toward us; behind her a color transparency depicts, in the manner of a movie back-projection, a four-lane highway bordered by telegraph poles extending toward a vanishing point on a hilly horizon. It seems to me that the opening of Aldrich's film where the hero encounters a woman (Christine, played by Cloris Leachman), naked under her raincoat, running down the road, influenced Cindy Sherman's composition to some degree.

Mention should also be made of Fritz Lang's attitude to architecture and its symbolic power. On his first trip to the United States, Lang was struck, like many other European travelers before him (Paul Bourget, Louis-Ferdinand Céline, Paul Morand, etc.), by the skyscrapers of New York and Chicago. It is clear that this archetypically American architecture – all at once majestic and intimidating, functional and symbolical – was for Lang a pure expression of modernist or futurist fascination with the idea of control, manipulation and mastery by powerful interests. Dr. Mabuse was a concentrated expression of these fantasies, which seem to have been shared by Lang himself. *Metropolis* (1927) clearly bears the stamp of these American impressions, with its connecting of silhouettes of skyscrapers to biblical images of *hubris* and of the Tower of Babel. One finds the same symbolism, which in the interim had become familiar and fully "Americanized," in the corporate buildings of *The Big Heat* or *While the City Sleeps*, where the action takes place in deliberately nameless cities. (This is a procedure I have referred to as "allegorical.") But, what happens when the action is set in Los Angeles? In the credits of *The Blue Gardenia*, a single drawn skyscraper symbolizes the metropolis; I think it depicts Los Angeles City Hall, that strange building whose pinnacle in the form of a step pyramid – like the tower of the Hawksmoor-designed St. George's Church in Bloomsbury (1731) – was inspired by the Mausoleum at Halicarnassus. However, neither the building nor the city thus represented is as immediately recognizable (except for Angelenos) as New York (or rather, Manhattan), San Francisco, or even Chicago. Nevertheless, the image is important as an instance of the Langian *leitmotif* that equates Modernist architecture, power, and America, even in Los Angeles whose landscape is so utterly distinct from New York and Chicago's. (The pyramidal form of City Hall also allows Lang to recall a classical past – whether Biblical, Egyptian, Babylonian, or Greek – that has survived or has been revived in the architecture of the twentieth century.) Ridley Scott, another Englishman exiled in Hollywood, set *Blade Runner* in a Los Angeles that is both futurist (with numerous echoes of Lang's *Metropolis*: airborne vehicles, Tower of Babel imagery) and full of ruins.

The Langian leitmotif of the skyscraper also tackles the problem of figuring verticality in film. Andersen, by stressing the verticality of film, would seem to neglect the panoramic formats, such as Cinema-Scope, and more generally the difficulty of representing height on screen; the horizontal or "Riemannian" format seems rather more suited to the Los Angeles landscape and to the architecture of Frank Lloyd Wright than it is to that of *The Fountainhead*, for instance. (Despite being an adaptation of Ayn Rand's novel, itself inspired by the biography of Frank Lloyd Wright, this King Vidor masterpiece attributes buildings to "Howard Roark" buildings that owe more to the proud functionalism of the Chicago skyscraper than they do to the horizontal lines of Wright in particular and the Prairy School in general).

Whether filmed on sets or on location, many films set in Los Angeles have a weirdly familiar quality. Take for instance the railway setting in which the criminal couple (played by Barbara Stanwyck and Fred MacMurray) dispose of Dietrichson's corpse in *Double*

Indemnity, or better still the magnificent location of Frank Tuttle's *This Gun for Hire*. In the latter film, which brought Alan Ladd and Veronica Lake together for the first time, the action begins in San Francisco before moving to Los Angeles, where a gigantic industrial landscape of railways and gasworks dwarfs the Alan Ladd character, producing an almost surreal "Incredible Shrinking Man" effect and highlighting the both derisory and pathetic weakness of the killer. In his first film, *The Salvation Hunters* (1925), Josef von Sternberg, usually considered a master of artifice, combines on-location shooting (San Pedro, Chinatown, the San Fernando Valley) and studio-shot scenes to create, with images of a dredger tirelessly clearing a canal of its mud, a documentary feel that also manages to exude a poetic strangeness. We find the same effect some sixty years later the oil derricks shown in one of Bill Viola's first videos, *Anthem* (1983), which was filmed in Long Beach and the Los Angeles Amtrak station (the video was first shown at the *Los Angeles 1955–1985: Naissance d'une capitale artistique* exhibition at the Pompidou Center in Paris from March to July 2006).

This does not mean that there are no positive, pastoral, or idyllic images of Los Angeles. Let's take *film noir* and the mythic couple of Alan Ladd-Veronica Lake again, this time in George Marshall's *The Blue Dahlia* (1946). Veronica Lake drives into the movie to act as Alan Ladd's compassionate guardian angel, a sort of anti-femme fatale, and if the rainy nocturnal setting seems stereotypically *noir*ish, the fact that the action takes place against the backdrop of the Pacific Ocean lends an aura of melancholy romanticism. Quite the opposite happens in Michael Curtiz's *Mildred Pierce*, where the Pacific, associated thematically with the evil Hispanic character, Monty Beragon (played by Zachary Scott), and with the murderous drives that propel Mildred (Joan Crawford) and her daughter Veda (Ann Blyth), exacerbates the noir and tragic aspects of the film: if the backdrop contributes to the general atmosphere of the film, it is also the case that the film's *genre* or mood tends to color the scenery. The thematic and visual motif linking the Pacific to the suicide of a character appears spectacularly in Cukor's *A Star is Born* as well as in *The Long Goodbye* by Altman.

Also deserving of mention in this respect is the magnificent, and decidedly un-*noir* melodrama, *Strangers When We Meet*, the story of an adultery, as passionate as it is shortlived, between an architect (Kirk Douglas) and a young woman (Kim Novak). In a clear parallel to the love affair, the architect builds a "house on the hill" for his writer client that represents the ideal and dream of an impossible love. This dwelling combines a rather horizontal, Japanese-influenced architecture evocative of Frank Lloyd Wright with the classical associations of elevation. (Here we should also mention the panoramic views of Los Angeles in *Mulholland Drive*, for example, or the aerial shots and breathtaking helicopter ballet at the opening of *Short Cuts*; an aerial view that, of course, is utterly different to those of New York that appear at the beginning Jules Dassin's *The Naked City* or Billy Wilder's *The Apartment*). The well-ordered suburbs of *Strangers When We Met*, like those of *Rebel Without a Cause*, also conceal a variety of sordid secrets, but they are domestic secrets rather than the crime and corruption we find in Chandler, for instance. The scenes where Kirk Douglas and Kim Novak meet in the restaurant on the edge of the Pacific, albeit more intimate and less spectacular, are on a par with the lyricism of *Vertigo*.

This rapid overview leads me to two related conclusions. The first is that the filmic representation of the urban space of Los Angeles is quite distinct from that of New York, Paris, London, Moscow, or San Francisco. In each of the latter cases, a single establishing shot is all that is required to identify the city: in New York's case, the southern tip of Manhattan seen from a boat, or the whole seen from a plane, with its easily recognizable landmarks – the Empire State Building, Chrysler Building, Brooklyn Bridge, and, until 2001, the Twin Towers of The World Trade Center; in the case of the other cities, the Eiffel Tower, Big Ben, Red Square and the Kremlin, the Golden Gate Bridge... Los Angeles City Hall does not enjoy a comparable "level of notoriety." The clichés that evoke (occasionally in a sarcastic vein) California are not architectural: there are orange groves (Norman Z. McLeod's *It's a Gift* with W.C. Fields, John Ford's *Grapes of Wrath*), the climate (the expression "In sunny California," frequently followed by a shot of torrential rain), as in the Tex Avery cartoons or *There's Always Tomorrow* by Douglas Sirk. California's image is thus pastoral, but one that is liable to reversal, whether simply through depiction of the flipside (thus, in Michael Curtiz's *Young Man with a Horn*, the Californian landscape is reduced to railways and gasworks); or a realization that this image is a fallacy; as demonstrated endlessly in the *noir* genre as well as films on Hollywood, with their "dream settings" of stars lounging around pools.

The idea that European exiles have a distinctive perception, hence a distinctive way of representing Los Angeles is seductive, but hard to substantiate. Michelangelo Antonioni's vision in *Zabriskie Point* is undoubtedly "European," its landscape of "signs" (billboards and publicity images) seemingly replacing the "reality" of things. This vision looks forward to Wim Wenders' clearly ironically-titled *Land of Plenty*. (Wenders' other debt to Antonioni, or at least the other common point in these films is the impression that the sprawling metropolis is totally hemmed in by desert.)

The Englishman John Boorman's experience of shooting his first American film, *Point Blank*, a *neo-noir*, is also noteworthy. First of all, he moved the action from San Francisco to Los Angeles because the type of film he wanted to make ("bleak, cold") could not take place among the pastel-colored Victorian houses of San Francisco; instead, he chose the "empty arid spaces" of Los Angeles. Next, he refused to use MGM's location department, which he accused of laziness in always choosing the same places ("the most convenient ones because they know the police will make things easy by blocking of this or that street"). He did his own scouting by helicopter and car, unearthing locations such as a dried-up canal that allowed him to convey his own vision of Los Angeles: disorienting, disconcerting, off-putting.

With Billy Wilder it is even easier to make: the elements of social satire are evident, but this satire does not owe everything to the director's European origins. Like many Hollywood productions, notably *noir* thrillers, Wilder's films are not only collective enterprises, but also issue from a process of hybridization in which storylines, characters, visual leitmotifs, urban architecture, lighting, framing, not to mention musical scores, draw on indigenous as well as German (or European) sources and reminiscences.

Finally, it should be remembered that, far from arousing a universally critical response, America's landscapes, whether urban or natural, awoke curiosity, interest, and even tenderness in the breasts of many European exiles. Wenders' feelings with regard to Los Angeles, and America in general, are clearly ambivalent: fascination mixed with repulsion and disappointed love... Contrasting two ways of seeing – one American, the other foreign – is too schematic and does not bear scrutiny. Furthermore, this fact is confirmed by the aforementioned exhibition at the Pompidou Center: the image of a Los Angeles of villas and swimming pools in the work of David Hockney tends toward the idyllic, while the "tableaux vivants" by the American Ed Kienholz, clearly inspired by the gothic tradition and Hollywood action movies, have a markedly trashy character.

Bibliographical Note

For those interested in the key role played by Los Angeles in the development of *film noir*, the place to start is James Naremore's *More than Night: Film Noir in Its Contexts* (Los Angeles, London and Berkeley: University of California Press, 1998); as well as Alain Silver and James Ursini's *L.A. Noir: The City as Character* (Santa Monica: Santa Monica Press, 2005) whose cover has a photo of the set of *The Crimson Kimono* by Samuel Fuller, with City Hall in the background.

On the making of *Point Blank*: John Boorman, *Adventures of a Suburban Boy* (London and New York: Faber and Faber, 2003); Michel Ciment's interview with Boorman, in *Boorman: un visionnaire en son temps* (Paris: Calmann-Lévy, 1985).

Translated by Colin Keaveney

© RMcN

ROBERT CROSSON | *The Day Sam Goldwyn*
Stepped Off The Train

inside wot? he thot, incorruptible?
no films that long anyway except gone with the wind
best known as a martha raye song when she sung jazz
or the wizard of oz & we all know where that went.
boxoffice gold brick roads did vast service to.

put moons in skies where there ws none
& turned stanford's pig's-ear into a goldmine
a fool a minute dont give a sucker an even break
them bad years people wanted ginger rogers to believe in
flying down to anyplace without an airticket
free for a dime with taps and dancing girls
on the wings.

class my ass,
try canoeing the colorado rapids without an oar
up at dawn to get the sun right (inside wot? he thot
incorruptible) coming back to the tent at night
too tired to get dressed for dinner.

Chapter One

The letters come to me by accident.
A friend needed cash & sold them at a bargain.

This was history, I told myself (money maybe,
but you don't kiss nobody's ass for nothing):
how the hell to make a story of it? Who thē
Sam Goldwyn, which the Muybridge? Letters lied.
Maybe a movie. Pictures made sense, I sez to myself,
who needs to read? That horse-trotting ws Stanford,
governor of California: you can't prove horses race
all fours off the ground, you don't get yr paycheck.
Was the railroad made it happen.
Houdini cdnt done better.
        To hell with the chinamen.

        as the man sez: talk straight
        straight man or chorus line stand on that rock
        Or a morning, out there waiting no chink would crow to
        one picture is worth ten-thousand crackups fly
        upsidedown

        try barreling off niagra on a sled sometime
        once across the border they want to see yr emigration
        papers.

        hortense powdermaker you needed, let's face it
        all you have to do is look at neveda city
        dickens over from england and read mark twain
        embellishing the frog, likewise left happy wife
        & family (in a photograph

        stood on that damned mountain half the morning
        & had to work with glass

        the 49th parallel is a high rock with a guy standing
        in leggings and boots
        a young uncle hanged with his shoes tied

all you have to do is look at nevada city
first concession of course is to discount literacy
carnegie did it with steel mills
inside wot? he thot
(cantering

Chapter Two
One has to be careful here.
The 49th parallel is a high rock with a guy in leggings
and boots. This photograph was shot at 6:30 AM without
breakfast.

twelve fools a minute saddled up that boardwalk
incorruptible? big bucks is where the country goes
a man needs vision.

dickens read mark twain with a high rock standing
you riding across them plains in a smoker
never once bothered to look out the window

first-class letters posted sentence & paragraph
them guys knew where the buck is
they built the railroad

mud and mosquitoes
four-mile trestles with ties and trackbed
read up & down

all chinamen.

Scene Three

Died.
Day after the war, Willie-Rose-Bud Hearst
opens east wing of his Roman swimming pool.
A man is shot, boat capsizes: Esther Williams
opens another restaurant, helicopters can't get in.
Giraffes rampage the lumberyard.

> Hortense Powdermaker reads Mark Twain
> embellishing the frog left happy wife
> and family in a photograph
> his granddaughter wound up
> at Arms Hotel on Highland Avenue.

Synopsis

Sam runs for mayor: Muybridge supports.
Chinese restaurants become unfashionable. Health-
food stores proliferate... Eastman Kodak turns its
back. Sam wins by a narrow margin... Police on horse-
back run down whores on Sunset Boulevard... Sam is
shot. The pope rallies. Iranians take over Beverly
Hills. The City Council disbands streetcars; in-
cinerators become a bond issue. Sam writes a musical.
People are ransomed at airports. Burbank housewives
are flown to Rochester. Political candidates support
harpsichord concerts. Theater owners host barbeques
in back yards. Kodak wins. Sam, run out as an entertainer,
retires to the Valley. His rock opera is a success.

nina gabrilowitsch is found dead on somebody's
front steps in laguna.

kennedy dies, Weyerhauser plants trees.
everybody jogs

Contributors' Notes

BRUCE BÉGOUT, former student of the Ecole Normale Supérieure Ulm, holder of the *Agrégation* and Doctor in Philosophy, he is Assistant Professor at the Université Bordeaux-III. He has authored many books, among them *Zéropolis, l'expérience de Las Vegas* (Paris: Allia, 2002), *Lieu commun, le motel américain* (Paris: Allia 2003) and *L'Eblouissement des bords de route* (Paris: Verticales, 2004). He is currently working on a book about Los Angeles (*La ville provisoire*), which will be a syntheses of his philosophical research on suburban America.

Poet/translator GUY BENNETT is the author of four collections of poetry, most recently *Drive to Cluster* (Piacenza, Italy: ML & NLF, 2003), and, with Béatrice Mousli, of *Poésies des deux mondes: un dialogue franco-américain à travers les revues, 1850–2004* (Paris: Ent'revues, 2004). His poems have appeared in magazines and anthologies internationally, and his translations include works by Nicole Brossard, Jean-Michel Espitallier, Mostafa Nissabouri, Valère Novarina, Jacques Roubaud, and Giovanna Sandri. Bennett is the publisher of Seeing Eye Books, co-editor of Seismicity Editions, and is a contributing editor to the *New Review of Literature* (USA) and *Électron Libre* (Morocco). He lives in Los Angeles, and teaches at Otis College of Art and Design.

JEAN-LOUP BOURGET is professor of cinema studies at the Ecole Normale Supérieure and author of numerous books on cinema and Hollywood. Among the most recent, *Les Européens à Hollywood* (Paris: Armand Colin, 2006), *Hollywood, la norme et la marge* (Paris: Armand Colin, 2005), *Le Mélodrame Hollywoodien* (Paris: Ramsay, 1994), *John Ford* (Paris: Rivages, 1990).

MICHEL BULTEAU participated, in 1971, in the *Manifeste Électrique*. He is the author of numerous books of poetry & prose, including *Ether-mouth, slit, hypodermique* (1974), *Des siècles de folie dans le calèches étroites* (1976), *Les Iles des eaux* (1982, 1997), *Flowers* (1989), *Poèmes 1966–1974* (1993), *L'effrayeur* (2000), *Sérénité moyenne (poèmes 1990–1996)* (2000), and most recently, *Un héros de New York ou Comment je me suis donné au diable* (Paris: la Différence, 2003).

Born in Canonsburg, Pennsylvania in 1929, ROBERT CROSSON moved to California with his family in 1944. He eventually settled in Los Angeles where he spent most of his life, working as a carpenter, house painter, and professional actor. The author of four volumes of poetry – *Geographies, Abandoned Latitudes* (with John Thomas and Paul Vangelisti), *Calliope, The Blue Soprano, The Day Sam Goldwyn Stepped Off the Train* – and the chapbook *In The Aethers of the Amazon.* Robert Crosson died in 2001.

SOPHIE DANNENMÜLLER is an independent scholar specializing in California art. She has written and lectured about California art and California artists such as Wallace Berman and George Herms in both the United States and France. She recently worked as a researcher and exhibition assistant at the Pompidou Center in Paris for the *Los Angeles, 1955–1985* exhibition of 2006, and is currently writing a history of assemblage art in California for a doctorate in art history at the Sorbonne. She lives in France.

Born in 1957, JEAN-MICHEL ESPITALLIER is the author of numerous books of poetry, most recently *En guerre* (Paris: Inventions/Inventaire, 2004), editor of *Pièces détachées, une anthologie de la poésie française aujourd'hui* (Paris: Pocket, 2000), and author of the study *Caisse à outils, un panorama de la poésie française aujourd'hui* (Paris: Pocket, 2006). In 1989 he co-founded the award-winning magazine *Java*, which ceased publication after fifteen years of activity. A translation of his *Fantasy bouchère* [*Butcher Fantasy*] was published by Duration Press in 2004, and his *Théorème d'Espitallier* [*Espitallier's Theorem*], translated by Guy Bennett, was published by Seismicity Editions in Spring 2005.

Born in 1966, CHRISTOPHE FIAT lives in Paris, where, after a brief career teaching philosophy, he now devotes his time to poetry and performance. Co-founder of the magazine *The Incredible Justine's Adventures,* Fiat's publications include *New York 2001, Poésie au galop* (Paris: Al Dante, 2002), *Ritournelle, une anti théorie* (Paris: Al Dante, 2002) *Bienvenus à Sexpol* (Paris: Leo Scheer, 2003) *Qui veut la peau de Harry ?* (Paris: Inventaire/Invention, 2004) and *Epopée, une aventure de Batman à Gotham City* (Paris: Al Dante/Niok, 2004).

CYNTHIA GHORRA-GOBIN, geographer and specialized in American studies, is research director at CNRS (Centre national de la recherche scientifique). She has a Ph.D in Literature from the Paris 1 University, and a Ph.D in Urban Planning from UCLA. She teaches at the Institut d'Etudes Politiques in Paris and at Paris IV-Sorbonne. She works on the social, cultural and political changes of the city in the context of globalization. Her most recent works are *Los Angeles, le mythe américain inachevé,* (Paris: CNRS éditions, 1997 & 2002) (Prix France-Amériques), *Les Etats-Unis entre local et mondial,* (Paris: Presses de Sciences Po, 2000) and *Villes et société américaine,* (Paris: Armand Colin, 2003).

HAL GLICKSMAN was born in Beverly Hills in 1937. An art instructor at California State University, in Long Beach, he has directed many galleries and art spaces in Southern California, including the Art Gallery of Otis Art Institute where he exhibited Sam Francis, Louis Kahn and Richard Mock. He has authored many essays and catalogs and is now retired and living in the Normandie region of France.

JOHN HUMBLE received a BA in philosophy from the University of Maryland and an MFA from the San Francisco Art Institute. His large-scale color photographs of the ironies and paradoxes of the Los Angeles landscape have been exhibited and published internationally. His work is in numerous collections including the Corcoran Gallery of Art, the National Museum of American Art, the Smithsonian Institute, the Library of Congress, LACMA, the San Francisco Museum of Modern Art, and the J. Paul Getty Museum. In addition to making fine-art photographs of the L.A. landscape, he has also done editorial work for *Time, Newsweek, U.S. News and World Report, Elle, The Los Angeles Times Magazine, Harper's, Esquire,* and *Geo.* He is represented by the Jan Kesner Gallery in Los Angeles. In March 2007, the J. Paul Getty Museum exhibited and published a book of John Humble's photographs of the Los Angeles landscape and the Los Angeles River entitled, *A Place in the Sun.*

DAVID JAMES who, in the 1970s published two chapbooks in and about Los Angeles, as well as giving many poetry readings and contributing to *Invisible City* and other poetry journals. More recently he has been teaching in the School of Cinema-Television at the University of Southern California, and writing about non- and anti-corporate film and other forms of culture in the city. James is the author of *Allegories of Cinema: American Film in the Sixties* (Princeton University Press, 1989), *Power Misses: Essays Across (Un)Popular Culture* (London: Verso Books, 1996), and *The Most Typical Avant-Garde: History and Geography of Minor Cinemas in Los Angeles* (University of California Press, 2006). He also edited *To Free the Cinema: Jonas Mekas and the New York Underground* (Princeton University Press, 1992), *The Hidden Foundation: Cinema and the Question of Class* (Minnesota University Press, 1996), *The Sons and Daughters of Los: Culture and Community in L.A.* (Temple University Press, 2003), and *Stan Brakhage: Filmmaker* (Temple University Press, 2006).

NORMAN KLEIN is a cultural critic, and both an urban and media historian, as well as a novelist. His books include *The History of Forgetting: Los Angeles and the Erasure of Memory, Seven Minutes: The Life and Death of the American Animated Cartoon,* the data/cinematic novel, *Bleeding Through: Layers of Los Angeles, 1920–86* (DVD-ROM with book), *The Vatican to Vegas: The History of Special Effects"* (New York: The New

Press, 2005), and *Freud in Coney Island* (Los Angeles: Seismicity Editions, 2006). His essays appear in anthologies, museum catalogs, newspapers, scholarly journals, on the web – symptoms of a polymath's career – and range in their subject matter from European cultural history to animation and architectural studies, from L.A. studies to fiction, media design, and documentary film. His work, which includes museum shows, centers on the relationship between collective memory and power, is usually set in urban spaces, and often straddles the thin line between fact and fiction in its exploration of erasure, forgetting, scripted spaces, and the social imaginary.

BILL KROHN has been since 1978 the Hollywood correspondent for *Les Cahiers du cinéma. Les Cahiers* recently published his book *Hitchcock au travail,* which Phaidon Press will publish in English this spring as *Hitchcock at Work. Hitchcock au travail* won the French Critics Association prize for Best Large-Format Book of 1999. Krohn also edited, for Cahiers and the Locarno film festival, *Joe Dante et les gremlins d'Hollywood.* In 1993 he co-wrote, -directed, and -produced *It's all true,* based on an unfinished film by Orson Welles. He is currently completing a documentary about the 1947 Roswell incident for release on the Internet.

BÉATRICE MOUSLI is the author of numerous books, among them *Intentions, histoire d'une revue littéraire des années vingt* (Paris: Ent'revues 1996), *Les Editions du Sagittaire 1919–1979* (Paris: IMEC, 2003), *Valery Larbaud* (Paris: Flammarion, 1998, Grand Prix de la Biographie de l'Académie Française), *Virginia Woolf* (Paris: Ed. du Rocher, 2001), *Max Jacob* (Paris: Flammarion, 2005, Prix Anna de Noailles 2006 de l'Académie Française). With her husband Guy Bennett, she wrote *Charting the Here of There: French & American Poetry in Translation published in literary magazines (1850–2002)* (Granary Books, 2002; French translation Ent'revues, 2004), and they have curated the exhibits "Reviews of Two Worlds; French and American Literary Periodicals, 1945–2002" at the New York Public Library (Fall 2002), "Charting the Here of There: A French and American Dialogue in Poetry" at the Doheny Memorial Library at the University of Southern California (Spring 2003). They have also organized several conferences, among which "Review of Two Worlds", (USC-Otis College of Art and Design, 2003), and "Los Angeles, A Different Look at a Different City," at the Bibliothèque Nationale de France (Paris, June 2006).

MARTHA RONK is the author of several books of poetry, most recently *Why/Why Not* (University of California Press) and *In a Landscape of Having to Repeat.* She is also the author of a memoir, *Displeasure of the Table* (Sun & Moon). Her chapbooks include *Prepositional* (Seeing Eye Books) and *Quotidian* (a+bend books). Her collaborations include *Allegory* (Italy ML & NLF), with the artist Tom Wudl and *Desert Geometries* (Littoral Books) with the artist Don Suggs. She is the Irma & Jay Price Professor of English at Occidental College and co-poetry editor for the *New Review of Literature*. She lives in Los Angeles.

KEVIN STARR, University Professor and professor of history at the University of Southern California and California State Librarian Emeritus, was born in San Francisco in 1940. After graduation from the University of San Francisco in 1962, Starr served two years as a lieutenant in a tank battalion in Germany. Upon release from the service, Starr entered Harvard University where he took his MA degree in 1965 and his Ph.D. in 1969 in American Literature. He also holds the Master of Library Science degree from UC Berkeley and has done post-doctoral work at the Graduate Theological Union. Starr has served as Allston Burr Senior Tutor in Eliot House at Harvard, executive assistant to the Mayor of San Francisco, the City Librarian of San Francisco, a daily columnist for the San Francisco *Examiner,* and a contributing editor to the *Opinion* section of the Los Angeles *Times.* The author of numerous newspaper and magazine articles, Starr has written and/or edited fourteen books, six of which are part of his *American and the California Dream* series. His writing has won him a Guggenheim Fellowship, membership in the Society of American Historians, and the Gold Medal of the Commonwealth Club of California. His most recent book is *California, A History* (Random House, 2005).

PAUL VANGELISTI is the author of some twenty books of poetry, as well as being a noted translator from Italian. His new collection, *Days Shadows Pass,* has just been published by Green Integer Books. Most recently, his and Lucia Re's translation of Amelia Rosselli's *War Variations* (Green Integer, 2005) won the 2006 Premio Enzo Flaiano in Italy and the 2006 PEN-USA Award for Translation. From 1971–1982 he was co-editor, with John McBride, of the literary magazine *Invisible City* and, from 1993–2002, edited *Ribot,* the annual publication of the College of Neglected Science. Curently, with Luigi Ballerini, he is editing a five-volume anthology of U.S. poetry from 1960 to the present, *Nuova poesia americana,* for Mondadori in Milan. Paul Vangelisti is Founding Chair of the Graduate Writing program at Otis College of Art & Design.

D.J. WALDIE is the author of *Holy Land: A Suburban Memoir* (1996, Norton; revised 2005), *Real City: Downtown Los Angeles Inside/Out* (2001, Angel City), *Where We Are Now: Notes from Los Angeles* (2004, Angel City), and *Close to Home: An American Album* (2004, Getty Museum). His narratives about life in Los Angeles have appeared in the *Kenyon Review, Salon* (the Internet magazine), *dwell, Los Angeles Magazine,*

Bauwelt, and other publications. He is a contributing writer at *Los Angeles Magazine*, and his book reviews and commentary appear in the *Los Angeles Times* and the *New York Times*. Waldie has also lectured on the social history of southern California at the campuses of the University of California Irvine, San Diego, Davis, and UCLA; Cal Tech; the Southern California Institute of Architecture; the Art Center College of Design, and the University of Maryland, among other institutions; and he delivered the Haynes Foundation Lecture at the Huntington Library in 2003. Waldie has been the Public Information Officer of the city of Lakewood since 1978. He received an MA in Comparative Literature from UC Irvine in 1974. He lives a not-quite-middle-class life in Lakewood, in the house his parents bought in 1946.